The
Courage
Companion

The Courage Companion

How to Live Life With True Power

By Nina Lesowitz and Mary Beth Sammons

VIVA
EDITIONS

Published in the United States by Viva Editions, an imprint of Cleis Press Inc., 2246 Sixth Street, Berkeley, California 94710.

Printed in the United States.
Cover design: Scott Idleman
Cover photograph: Siede Preis/Getty Images
Text design: Frank Wiedemann
10 9 8 7 6 5 4 3 2 1

ISBN: 978-1-57344-409-5

Library of Congress Cataloging-in-Publication Data

Lesowitz, Nina.
 The courage companion : how to live life with true power / Nina Lesowitz and Mary Beth Sammons.
     p. cm.
 ISBN 978-1-57344-409-5 (trade paper : alk. paper)
1. Courage. 2. Courage--Case studies. 3. Conduct of life--Case studies. I. Sammons, Mary Beth. II. Title.
 BJ1533.C8L47 2010
 179'.6--dc22
                                        2010028094

To my beloved late mother, Tomoko, who faced her challenges with grace and fortitude. Mom, you were the personification of courage and remain my biggest inspiration.

—Nina Lesowitz

To my mother, Isabel McMahon Von Driska, who taught me by example that the greatest form of courage is to initiate each and every action with kindness toward others. When we think about doing unto others first, we forget to be afraid.

—Mary Beth Sammons

TABLE OF CONTENTS

FOREWORD BY LARRY COX

The courage celebrated in this book comes in many forms. Whether a selfless act to protect others, a call to conscience, a fight against injustice, or a struggle to reach a personal goal, the human stories included in this volume inspire us, teach us, and remind us that courage is, as Winston Churchill said, the *first* of human qualities because it is the quality which guarantees all others.

In my work as a human rights advocate, activist, and leader of Amnesty International, I have been privileged to witness acts of courage by brave men and women around the globe. Many of these individuals burn with determination to stand up for what is right. They are willing to—

and often do—endure arrest, abuse, intimidation, torture, even death to fight injustice and oppression. Often, these are bold acts of courage that make global headlines, like the thousands of protesters who took to the streets in Iran following the disputed 2009 presidential election and were subjected to terrifying assaults by a regime trying desperately to hold on to power.

Courageous leaders who have stood up throughout history to protect and advance human rights and principles inspire our deepest admiration. Millions have been inspired by Dr. Martin Luther King and the Burmese democracy activist and prisoner of conscience Daw Aung San Suu Kyi, whose story is highlighted in this volume. Their stories of courageous leadership are powerful examples of the human determination to achieve freedom and protect human rights. We owe leaders like Dr. King and Suu Kyi—along with their unsung and brave followers—our gratitude and a willingness to support, in ways either small or large, public or private, the cause that inspired them.

This book profiles individuals who today are fighting injustice amid threats, harassment, and violence. Their courage is often breathtaking. Women of Zimbabwe Arise, led by Jenni Williams and Magodonga Mahlangu, have been harassed, intimidated, beaten, and jailed by authorities for their fight against Zimbabwe's worsening social, economic, and human rights abuses. Rita Mahato has been threatened with death, rape, and kidnapping to help women in Nepal who have suffered acts of violence.

Shadi Sadr, an Iranian journalist and human rights lawyer, advocates for women's rights and fights the practice of stoning. Despite her arrest in 2009 following the presidential election and the authorities' closing of her legal advice center for women, she continues to espouse women's rights efforts through the website Women in Iran. The story of murdered journalist Anna Politkovskaya, who exposed brutality and corruption by state authorities in Russia, reminds us that the cost of fighting injustice may be life itself.

This book also calls attention to the quiet courage of individuals whose achievements, often no less stunning, take place out of the spotlight. They teach us a powerful lesson—that ordinary people whose names go unheralded can summon the courage and commitment to persevere toward a dream, help to right a wrong, or survive against odds. Their stories are deeply humbling.

Maddy Oden is a Californian who speaks out against the risk of inducing labor and unnecessary caesarean sections. Oden formed a foundation devoted to publicizing these concerns and preventing women from dying in childbirth after her only daughter, Tatia Oden French, 32, who was in perfect health and had no problems during her pregnancy, died needlessly with her infant child after she was given drugs to induce labor. Like so many others profiled in this book, Maddy Oden defines what it means to be irrepressible, resilient, committed—in a word, fired up.

I have been honored to work with people who have dedicated their lives to advancing justice, along with political, economic, social, and cultural rights. Their work is essential. But the true lifeblood of the human rights movement—like all movements—derives from the power of ordinary people who crave a more just world and act with conviction to help bring it about.

This book shows all of us that one individual can make a difference, changing the course of their own lives or the lives of others through a willingness to take a stand, overcome fear, go forward and never back down.

Larry Cox is a veteran human rights advocate and executive director of Amnesty International USA

Amnesty International, winner of the Nobel Peace Prize, celebrates its 50th anniversary in 2011. With more than 2.2 million supporters, activists, and volunteers in 150-plus countries, Amnesty International investigates and exposes abuses, educates and mobilizes the public, and works to protect people wherever justice, freedom, truth, and dignity are denied.

INTRODUCTION

It is from numberless diverse acts of courage and belief that human history is shaped. Each time a man stands up for an ideal, or acts to improve the lot of others, or strikes out against injustice, he sends forth a tiny ripple of hope; and, crossing each other from a million different centers of energy and daring, those ripples build a current which can sweep down the mightiest walls of oppression and resistance.

—Robert F. Kennedy

Growing up, we were enthralled by tales of derring-do. As young girls and avid readers, we devoured the Nancy Drew series of books, read biographies of all the explorers, and our imaginations were ignited by Laura Ingalls Wilder's tales of growing up on the prairie, Pearl S. Buck's *The Good Earth*, the willful and determined Mary in *The Secret Garden*, and Jo in *Little Women*.

Later, learning about heroes such as Susan B. Anthony, Karen Silkwood, Oskar Schindler, Dian Fossey, Nelson Mandela, Rosa Parks, and so many more cemented our abiding admiration for courageous people who took huge risks to help make the world a better place for the rest of us.

To this day, one of our favorite genres remains true stories of adventurers who pushed past their fears in order to explode barriers, set records, and test the limits of what is possible.

It wasn't difficult to find tales of courage among our 21st-century compatriots. What we wanted to do in surfacing these stories was to get their advice about how to tap into—and hold on to—our inner strength when times get tough, and when we're feeling all alone.

Seems like everyone has a different take on what courage really is. Many of the people we've found to be the bravest insist that they did nothing more than stay in the race longer than everyone else, or donate a kidney for a loved one because it was the right thing to do. Over and over, people we interviewed for the book told us, "I don't really consider myself courageous."

So what is courage? And how do we get it? Where do we look for courage and how do we teach it to our children? These are questions we set out to explore as we tried to present a guide for readers to the ways courage surfaces in our modern world, and more importantly, how all of us can tap into it to find our true power.

What we discovered is that courage can be a form of tenaciousness, a refusal to quit because you're tired, or hurt, or humiliated, or emotionally broken. In fact, everyday courage is the ability to face what life throws in our path on a daily basis. What is that quality of mind or spirit that enables one person to face difficulty, danger, or pain without fear, or in the face of fear? What does it mean to have the courage of one's convictions?

Bravery implies the courage to face extreme dangers.

Certainly, heroic acts may be the first thing that comes to mind when envisioning courage—entering a burning building to save lives is one of the strongest images. And then there's that iconic image of the still-unidentified lone man who faced down the tanks of the Red Army during the massacre at Tiananmen Square.

Yes, those acts of bravery show us what courage *looks* like. But we wanted to understand what courage *feels* like. We interviewed people who have valiantly struggled to carry on following months of unemployment; the suicide of a loved one; deep depression; the end of a relationship;

moving to a new neighborhood; and people who found the confidence to try new things or stand up to a bully. Do you know how to really be brave?

Spiritual teacher and author Iyanla Vanzant says that courage comes by taking action before you are forced to. What about when we have difficulty engaging closely with others, especially our own family members or our employees? How do we cultivate courage to overcome a fear of intimacy? Where do we find the inspiration to face life's challenges or follow our dreams?

We found that courage, which we also call bravery, will, intrepidity, and fortitude, is the ability to confront fear, pain, risk, danger, uncertainty, or intimidation. Physical courage is courage in the face of physical pain, hardship, and threat of death. Moral courage is the ability to act rightly in the face of popular opposition, shame, or discouragement.

In this book, we take you into the living rooms, offices, and hospitals and onto the front lines where real people, by actions not words, show us what courage looks and *feels* like through their compelling and inspiring stories. We also offer tips on how to become courageous and tap into your own inner brave heart.

We all need the strength to pursue our dreams. In *The Courage Companion: How to Live Life With True Power,* we surface the stories of motivational and inspirational real-life ordinary people who in extraordinary ways have tapped into the courage and fortitude within. They inspire and remind us that whatever our fears, whatever the challenge of the moment, this too will pass. And perhaps most importantly, we serve up these stories of real people who have tapped into their courage to live their lives to their fullest. They become your guides, the inspiring individuals who hold your hand throughout the book to help you find the strength to "just do it."

May this book serve as a catalyst for your own courageous journey.

Peace,
Nina and Mary Beth

CHAPTER ONE
WHAT IS COURAGE?

We gain strength, and courage, and confidence by each experience in which we really stop to look fear in the face ... We must do that which we think we cannot.

—Eleanor Roosevelt

We live in times of unprecedented uncertainty. Failing to acknowledge this new reality means we live in denial and we risk fully living our lives and surviving the challenges that lie ahead of us.

Often our inability to know the future triggers the fight-or-flight response. We want to run and hide, or else panic sets in. That's because our minds want and seek certainty and security. So living in uncertainty feels a lot like the way we felt as children when we worried about the bogeyman we were certain lived in our closet. The only way we could accept that he was not there was to open that closet door.

Now especially, when millions of us live without health insurance, struggle to make house payments and pay bills, or fear that we will become ill or something terrible will happen to us, we need to embrace courage and tap into the inner power of living courageously. We need to reach deeper inside ourselves to draw from a well of fortitude, strength, and resiliency, and forge ahead with our inner closet doors open.

Living bravely today is all about reaching deep within for a quiet power that guides us through our inner fears and anxieties, and steadies and supports us against outside forces that threaten to shake our foundations. We need to learn how to transition gradually to this new way of thinking about courage.

In this chapter, and throughout the book, we have tried to focus on courage as seen through the lens of its origins. Courage comes from the Old French word *corage*, meaning heart, and spirit. We have collected stories and offered some of our own that are rooted in the kind of courage that comes from the power of our hearts and spirits, a power that when we manifest it makes the world a better place for ourselves and others.

In researching this book and going to the front lines of people who seem to be living boldly in these uncertain times, we observed that most of the people we interviewed shared one collective quality: Most insisted, "I am not courageous." In fact, they said they felt very afraid. But here's the key that separates those who take action in the face of their fears and those who stay frozen: Courageous people feel their fear but take action anyway. Courageous people admit to being afraid, but they deal with their fears and stand up to them.

Experts say the ability to tap into our courage is one of our most important qualities for success. And they say it is possible to teach ourselves to boost our courage quotient. Courageous people pay attention to the tiny little-engine-that-could voice inside them that says, "I think I can, I think I can," even when they are trembling in fear.

Our goal is not for you to eliminate fear, but to be able to transform it so that you can live fully in spite of it. If we can learn how to relax and reach deep within, we will find creativity, hope, and opportunity in our challenges. We want to introduce you to a team of people who are brimming with bravery, and teeming with verve.

SWEET SUCCESS: COURAGE SERVES UP TURN-AROUND OPPORTUNITIES FOR A COMMUNITY OF WOMEN IN THE FACE OF DESPAIR

Courage is looking fear right in the eye and saying, "Get the hell out of my way, I've got things to do."

—*Author unknown*

Across town from each other in Teaneck, New Jersey, two stories of monumentally difficult situations played out during the fall of 2009. At the height of the worst recession in decades, Angela Logan, a single mom of three, saved her home from foreclosure with a bake sale. Meanwhile, at Zoe's Cupcake Café, Miriam Bloom and Jane Fiedler were struggling to crank out some 300-plus cupcakes a day in their tiny shop, which doubles as a nonprofit organization that raises funds to help young teenage moms regain control of their lives, break cycles of poverty and abuse, and graduate from high school with a plan for the future.

4

Perhaps it was the climate of courage that formed the history of this river town which propelled these baking frenzies. What is certain is that these women fortified their efforts with dollops of bravery and staved off what could have been complete despair. In doing so they created turn-around opportunities for themselves and others.

We're certain that their stories belong alongside those throughout the history of this city of 40,000, where courage has marked its residents with a capital C. Teaneck is no stranger to momentous events that require tremendous acts of bravery. After the defeat at the Battle of Fort Washington, George Washington led his troops through Teaneck to escape the British Army. In the 1960s, Teaneck became the first community in the nation with a white majority to voluntarily desegregate public schools.

In all of their circumstances, from Angela's family facing the loss of their home, to the teens struggling to care for their newborns, to the duo of do-gooders who were trying to offer hope, the plight of these women might make you ask, How do they do it? Where do they find the guts to get out of bed in the morning and face futures that seem so uncertain? What does it feel like when you could lose your home, or you don't have a car, have a sick baby, and could lose your job because you can't afford to hire a baby-sitter? What keeps you going when it seems the world has your back up against the wall with nowhere to turn?

Certainly the idea of having to reach out to others

and admit despair and vulnerability seems terrifying to us. We think it is probably one of most people's greatest fears. That's where bravery stepped in for these women. Through their stories, we have learned that bravery is not about not *being afraid. It is about being afraid and forging ahead anyway, even when the world seems to be closing in. That is exactly what these women, and those they inspired, did at a time when most Americans were shaking in their boots with financial insecurity and an uncertain future. Their gutsy, go-getter attitudes invite us all to adopt a spirit of courageousness.*

"The baking was easy," Angela Logan recalls. "But it was *very* hard to have to ask people to buy the cakes and to tell them why. I just decided in the beginning that my pride was less important than saving my children and myself from losing our home. And so I swallowed my pride, smiled, mustered up my courage, and told people what had happened and how I needed their help. I just knew I had to do everything I could to help my family. I think it was probably the toughest thing I have ever had to do in my life."

In 2009, Logan began peeling apples and baking her family's favorite cake one at a time to stave off a threatened foreclosure after a contractor skipped out with the funds she had paid him for some remodeling and some acting gigs dried up when her actors agency shut its doors.

She named her delicacy "Mortgage Apple Cake" and sold 100 in 10 days at $40 apiece. The $4,000 allowed her to pay off some bills and qualify for a federal program to lower her monthly payments.

"It was a flash of desperation," Logan says. An actor who has done commercials and stand-up comedy and appeared on *Law & Order: Special Victims Unit*, Logan was also in school part-time looking to switch to nursing—steadier work than acting. "I thought, wow—we could sell these cakes, they're so good."

Angela's story of resourcefulness and guts was picked up by an obit writer at a the local weekly newspaper, then exploded in the national media limelight: NBC's *Today Show* and CNN. So did cake sales.

But operating her entrepreneurial effort out of her kitchen, "with just two pans," was her next challenge. That's when Miriam Bloom and Jane Fiedler reached out to Angela. The duo actually showed up on Angela's doorstep to offer their commercial baking facility and their sales staff to help her churn out and sell her apple cakes.

At the same time, Miriam and Jane were struggling with their own challenges, trying to get the funding to open a home for the teen mothers and their babies, and keep their nonprofit helping the dozens of desperate young women who contact them on their hotline from across the country. But in the midst of their own struggle they were moved by Angela's story and reached out to help.

"There on the TV was someone who was our neighbor, though we didn't know her at the time, but we had a kitchen and place to sell her cakes, so we thought, Why not," Miriam remembers.

Providence swooped in, with perhaps a little pinch of good karma, and in the fall of 2009 Zoe's Place (www. zoesplaceinc.com), the nonprofit that operates in conjunction with the cafe, received $100,000 in funding from Women United in Philanthropy, a Bergen County, New Jersey, organization.

"Most of the women are young mothers trying to do a good job," Jane, who helped bring the café to life, says. "They haven't done anything wrong." Zoe's Place established a helpline (973-458-1007) to provide information, advocacy, and support to the community. They have been inundated ever since with calls from teen moms and pregnant teens, and from care managers representing virtually every organization and agency in contact with the girls. Placing a call to the helpline is all a girl needs to do to obtain emergency services, information, or advocacy for herself and her child.

Still, Jane says, "People don't want to take a chance on them, or they don't have a great work history yet because they're seventeen." That's where the café comes in. Zoe's Cupcake Café hires the young mothers in jobs from bookkeeping to counter sales and management. (The name Zoe means "gift of life," Jane explains.) "These girls have dreams and hopes like everybody else," she says. "What they don't have is the belief that they can realize them."

Angela was immediately moved by the Zoe's Place mission. "In some ways, what Jane and Miriam are doing for these girls and what I was trying to do are one and the same. It was all about homes and a future for families. I decided after all I went through that if I got out, I would do everything I could do to help others. I was very impressed by what these women were doing for girls in desperate situations, trying to fight for a future for themselves and their children. I wanted to help."

Angela sold the license for her apple cake recipe to a New York–based Internet cake supplier, and these days she works at the cupcake shop developing new cake recipes and supporting the effort to help teenage mothers get a foothold in the workplace. (The New York company allows her to continue selling the cakes on her own as well.) Through the courage and resiliency of these female mentors—Angela, Miriam, and Jane—the young women and their babies are all getting a turnaround opportunity.

In addition to her cake-baking entrepreneurial efforts, Angela is looking into becoming a life coach, focusing on helping people who are having financial difficulties.

Courage is at the heart of what happened in Teaneck during the fall of 2009 and is what continues to drive the only chance these moms have for strong, healthy families and hopeful new beginnings.

"The story of courage here is the bravery of these girls and moms like Angela who have such amazing resiliency and have to call on everything inside themselves to put a roof over their children's heads," Jane says. "It takes a lot of courage when you are hurting and have to reach out to others and ask them to help you and trust that these people are good when others have hurt you so deeply. I have great respect for these women who can smile in the face of such anxiety and keep on going."

POWER PRACTICE
Jane recommends that at times when we want to throw in the towel and say "I just can't do it," we pause and think of Angela and these teen moms who wake up every morning to face their fears. We will be inspired by their courage. "The takeaway for all of us is to be inspired by their resilience and courage," she says.

COURAGE DOESN'T ALWAYS ROAR. SOMETIMES COURAGE IS THE LITTLE VOICE AT THE END OF THE DAY THAT SAYS, I'LL TRY AGAIN TOMORROW.

—Mary Anne Radmacher

• •• ● •• •

Conduct an Internet search for inspirational quotes, and Mary Anne Radmacher's beautiful words above are frequently cited. We decided to track her down to learn what inspires her. She is the author of *Lean Forward Into Your Life, Courage Doesn't Always Roar, Promises to Myself,* and other motivational books, and her words and art can be found around the world in homes, hospitals, offices, and schoolrooms. For five years, she has presented a writing program for inmates at a medium-security prison in Salem, Oregon. You can learn more about her on her website: www.maryanneradmacher.com.

"People confuse courage with bravery," Radmacher says. "In my life experience, courage is that quiet whisper, that voice at night that says, I will try again tomorrow." She describes how her work teaching prisoners has expanded her understanding of what it means to be courageous, to take a stand: "How do you measure the courage of a felon who has made a commitment to rehabilitation, who has changed his fundamental beliefs, but is still behind bars?"

To stand apart and be different takes an enormous amount of courage, according to Mary Anne. "In any captive population—daycare, eldercare, public schools, or prisons—when you choose to follow the courage of your convictions, when you don't succumb to peer pressure, you are labeled different, and there are often consequences for those differences. In prison, it may result in a punch in the face." She asks, "How many of us would be willing to make a declaration of our changes with such violent consequences?" This is what she means by her observation that "courage doesn't always roar." It may be simply choosing to march to the beat of a different drummer. "For a felon to say, 'I didn't get that right, and I want to do better,' and to show such enormous vulnerability is profoundly courageous," Mary Anne says.

We agree. Finding courage when we are most vulnerable is what having guts is truly about. We may not be incarcerated, but some of us are captive in prisons of our own making. Sometimes we are locked in a job or career where it takes courage to stand up for ourselves, or in a relationship where our souls are trapped—unless we have the guts to speak up and take action.

We ask you to think of places and situations where mustering courage will have its consequences. That is what courage is all about. It is speaking up and taking action, even when the world around us pressures us to stay silent.

TRIUMPH OF THE SPIRIT: INJURED MARINE OVERCOMES SEVERE FACIAL AND SPINAL INJURIES TO WALK—AND SMILE—AGAIN

I know God will not give me anything I can't handle. I just wish that He didn't trust me so much.

—Mother Teresa

As founder of DOCS (Doctors Offering Charitable Services), a group of humanitarian surgeons who transform the broken lives of patients suffering from the most severe deformities, Munish Batra MD has seen horrific injuries. He and his team of physicians at www.docscharity.com donate their surgical reconstruction to operate on last-chance patient cases, the ones that other physicians and medical professionals have given up on. They heal bodies and souls.

The San Diego–based doctors have worked their magic on disfigured children, a severely maimed possible amputee victim, and a woman shot in the face and shoulder with a shotgun by her "boyfriend," to name just some of the people who otherwise were unable to obtain treatment for disfiguring medical conditions and severe injuries.

Their work has been lauded in the international limelight. In May 2010, Dr. Batra and DOCS landed the team on The Oprah Winfrey Show for their work with a 28-year-old female patient born with a rare and extremely disfiguring genetic disorder. Ana Rodarte has had seven surgeries to remove the tumors that covered most of her face and made it increasingly impossible to breathe, eat, and see.

But of all his patients in his private practice (Coastal Plastic Surgeons, www.coastalplasticsurgeons.com), and in the almost nine years since the foundation was launched in 2002, Dr. Batra says there is one patient who epitomizes the definition of courage: Ian Grado is a former Marine whose face was literally torn off and who was left paralyzed after a terrible car accident. It was Ian who inspired Dr. Batra to rally his surgeon peers and launch DOCS.

"When I think of the definition of courage, I think of Ian," Dr. Batra says. "When I first saw him after the accident I didn't have much hope. He was never supposed to walk again, and his injuries were some of the worst I have ever seen. Every time he walks into my office today, I am overwhelmed. I look at him and know what courage means."

* * *

Ian Grado was a 21-year-old Marine stationed at Camp Pendleton when the car he was driving with three military peers careened off the road and down an embankment during a blinding rainstorm, rolling over, and over, and over again. Shattered glass and twisted metal is all that rescue workers saw when they arrived at the scene and found the four young Marines. Ian suffered the most serious of the injuries, with severe disfigurement to his face and skull, a collapsed lung, and spinal damage to his neck and back that left him paralyzed from the chest down.

The other Marines in the accident literally had to hold Ian's face in place until paramedics arrived.

On that night, April 7, 2001, Ian was airlifted to Scripps Memorial Hospital in La Jolla, California, where in the course of one week he would undergo nine surgeries while in a medically induced coma. He had titanium rods placed in his spine and bones to fuse damaged vertebrae; his ribs were removed to reconstruct his face, which had been peeled back with the loss of his right earlobe during the accident.

"One of the first memories I have after coming down from the morphine was of my mom explaining what had happened to me, that I had been in an accident and was basically paralyzed," Ian recalls. "I remember telling her, 'I don't want to be paralyzed.' "

It was a diagnosis he was determined to overcome. "I basically knew that I didn't want to settle for the way things were and the way most people and doctors were telling me I was going to end up," Ian says. "They were saying that I probably would not get much better, which at that point meant being in a wheelchair. I basically just ignored any limits that anyone imposed on me, sometimes doing things that I probably shouldn't have. I think I allowed myself to break down only once, for about ten minutes. I told myself, okay, that is all you get. I wanted to focus on recovery, not feeling sorry for myself."

A week later, he was transferred to a VA hospital in his hometown, Albuquerque, New Mexico, where he spent five months undergoing rigorous rehabilitation therapy.

"The determination instilled in me by the Marine Corps and the will to get back to my girlfriend"—now his wife—"in California is what drove me to get through rehab, learn to walk again, and deal with the obvious looks and stares received while out in public," Ian says. What gave him the will to survive and push through, he said, was his military "stoic" training, but also the girlfriend, Stephanie, he had just started dating a month before the accident.

But for the courage he needed, Ian says, "I prayed a lot. My faith really helped me make sense of everything that was happening around and to me. When I was a Marine I would find myself doing things just because they were difficult and I think that transferred over to my rehab.

When I was in rehab I would have extreme difficulty with the simplest tasks, like moving my foot. It was a strange experience trying your hardest to do something that you used to be able to do so easily. I would sometimes get angry at myself for not being able to perform certain tasks, and that made me want to do it even more."

Through it all, he says he always tried to keep things in perspective. "I remembered what my senior drill instructor in boot camp once told us: 'Things could be worse.' The way I looked at it, I had two choices: do nothing or do something. I think most people when faced with obstacles basically come to that fork in the road. For myself, I had already made that decision long before my accident. That is how I approach my life." During the time he was undergoing intense rehabilitation, Ian says he reached deep inside to call on his faith and the courage to go on.

"I was a team leader at the time of the accident, and I possibly would have gone to Afghanistan and definitely to Iraq," he says. "It may sound stupid to most people, but that will always be one of my biggest regrets. I would have liked to go, even though I probably would have hated every minute of it. Not going and supporting my team and fellow Marines really got to me while I was in rehab, and still does to this day.

"I had completely accepted that I would have to go through the rest of my life with the imperfections to my appearance as a result of my accident, and just thought of it as the price I had to pay to still be alive," Ian says. "I did notice little kids would stare or ask me what happened. The extent to which this bothered me varied. Most of the time I would just play the stereotypical tough, stoic Marine. But other times it would get to me."

During his rehabilitation, Ian stayed in contact with Dr. Munish Batra. "I was interested in finding out what my options were as far as follow-up surgery," Ian says. "He was always very supportive to me and my family during my initial surgeries and treatment immediately following the accident. I quickly realized that the likelihood of one, finding a doctor as talented as Dr. Batra, and two, funding the surgery were quickly becoming unrealistic. It was around this time that Dr. Batra informed me about the DOCS organization that he was in the process of starting up and asked if I would like to be considered as a possible patient. Of course I jumped at the opportunity."

Ian is now a 31-year-old husband and father. On July 29, 2006, he married Stephanie, whom Dr. Batra calls "a wonderful woman who stood by his side and helped him have the courage to stay focused to heal." The couple live in San Diego with their daughter, Gianna, who is one. Ian has returned to school and earned an engineering degree. Today he works in satellite communications for the federal government.

"I cannot thank the DOCS organization enough for what they have done for me and my family," Ian says.

"They gave me a second chance that I may not have had otherwise."

POWER PRACTICE

Throughout his ordeal, Ian Grado replayed the mantra of his Marine senior drill instructor, "Things could be worse." He then realized he had two choices: to do nothing or to do something. Sometimes when we are facing our worst fears, we believe we don't have the courage to find our way through, no matter what the fates deal us. When we step back and make the assessment that things could be worse, we can rally and forge ahead.

DOWNHILL ALL THE WAY: THE COURAGE TO BECOME AN OLYMPIAN

Courage is resistance to fear, mastery of fear—not absence of fear.

—Mark Twain

Imagine: You are at the starting gate, waiting for the words "Ten seconds, then go." Before you is the most technical alpine downhill racecourse in the world, at Aspen, Colorado, or the fastest speed course, at Sugarloaf, Maine. You know your body is about to go 70 mph on extremely steep, icy, and varied terrain. Seventeen-year-old Foreste Peterson, a ski racer and member of the Sugar Bowl Ski Team, has skied down these courses, racing against the best teenage female skiers in the world.

One of the world's most dangerous competitive sport events, alpine downhill ski racing requires not that you overcome fear, but that you learn how to use it to your advantage. Foreste has sacrificed a "normal" social life in pursuit of her Olympian dream—now realized—of being selected for the US Ski Team.

A resident of Berkeley, California—hours away from the nearest ski slopes—this committed and courageous high school student began skiing when she was two years old. Driven to compete, Foreste had won several elite FIS (International Ski Federation) races by age 16 after becoming the top American in 2008 at two world show-cases: Trofeo Topolino in Italy and the Whistler Cup in Canada. In 2009, the United States Ski and Snowboard Association awarded her the Willy Schaeffler Award as Best Junior 2, the Far West Ski Association bestowed on her the Jimmy Glass Outstanding Junior of the Year Award, and she was granted the Mayor's Award of Excellence in Academics and Sport by the City of Berkeley.

Some of her many racing highlights include winning the Overall Combined at J2 Nationals (15-16-year-old category) at Sugarloaf, Maine, then finding herself on the podium two weeks later at the 2010 US Nationals alongside many Olympians, as a top Junior in the Super Combined and Giant Slalom.

Foreste describes how the nerves and adrenaline have helped fuel her rise to the pinnacle of the sport: competing as a member of the elite women's alpine team with dreams of the 2014 Olympic Winter Games in Sochi, Russia.

* * *

Most of us will never know the extent of the "total adrenaline rush" described by Foreste Peterson when she is on the edge of a mountain, ready to race down a 73-degree slope. How does this teenager manage those feelings?

"I focus on the moment, I focus on my strength, I begin to breathe," Foreste says. "When I am in the starting gate, I don't actually feel much. I go numb. All of my focus is channeled into what will make me go as fast as possible for the next sixty seconds, give or take."

Foreste has a prerace routine that consists of a dynamic warm-up to get her muscles firing, and visualizing herself in the course executing all of the difficult sections. "Also, I put snow down my back a couple of minutes before I go," she relates. "This pumps me up more than anything." During her visualization, Foreste is confident knowing she can execute the next 1.5 minutes of, in her words, "going very fast."

In point of fact, when she races, she is traveling down a vertical drop at almost 70 mph. "When I am in race mode, I do not even let the word *scary* pop into my head," she says. "So instead of phrasing it this way, I like to say that some starts and what's to follow are just more challenging and more demanding than others." What makes them challenging and more demanding? "A really steep pitch, icy conditions, and the level of competition present at the race," she says.

Foreste attributes her skill and abilities to her early start in the sport, having been introduced to skiing at the tender age of two. Her parents, both avid skiers, compete in mountain biking, and her mother, Barbara Edelston Peterson, is a multi-time world champion in off-road triathlon. Foreste reports that they remain two of her biggest inspirations: "Most of my ski friends never ski with their parents because they can't stand waiting around so much. Fortunately, with the way my parents operate and the way they know how to ski, I do not have that problem. I feel so lucky to be blessed with athletic parents who not only keep up with me on the slopes, but support me in all of my endeavors."

She describes a "typical" week at home during ski season:

> Monday–Tuesday: Go to school in Berkeley, light workouts focused on recovery, lots of homework, always trying to catch up and get ahead when possible.
>
> Tuesday night: Drive three and a half hours from Berkeley to Lake Tahoe.
>
> Wednesday–Thursday: Train with team
>
> Friday–Sunday: Compete

During the evenings, she spends one and a half hours working on skis, reviewing videos after training or racing, and showering, eating, studying, and doing laundry. Many of the weeks are "away" weeks in Utah, Colorado, or on the East Coast, so the routine is completely different but filled with training, racing, ski tuning, video analysis, eating, homework, and sleeping very little. "Without a doubt, my schedule is intense and often very stressful," Foreste explains. "But all I can say is that the intensity and stress is so worth pursuing what I love to do best in life!"

In addition to dedication and athletic ability, it takes an enormous amount of bravery for someone to suppress her natural self-preservation instincts and throw herself fearlessly onto a dangerous course where mortal danger is a constant companion. Ski racers have to overcome fear to force their bodies to override instinct and learn new patterns of movement.

How is this learned? Foreste tells us that being coached for proper techniques over many years makes the difference. "Ski racing at the elite level requires technical development and superior fitness—there are specific ski racing techniques per event: slalom, giant slalom, super G, and downhill, and without the fitness to back it up, there is no way any athlete can be competitive and safe," she says.

Thankfully, Foreste has been relatively injury free. "I have had boot bang (shin splints) that has been challenging, and also a broken thumb," she says. "Friends have suffered major injuries, biggest being a severe head injury, but in general the injuries are intense knee problems or tibia fractures."

Not only is the sport Foreste competes in extremely dangerous, it is nerve-racking because results boil down to just one day, one hour, and one minute of concentration to be the fastest at that particular point.

Many of us dream of standing on that podium, representing our country, and being awarded the ultimate trophy—a coveted gold metal. The athletes like Foreste who train all their lives for an actual shot at that dream exemplify the true meaning of courage. The courage to try, and try again, takes a lot of heart, or *coer*, the root word of courage, which comes from the French and translates as "heart." It takes a lot of heart to refuse to quit because you're tired, have a bad day, or because the competition continues at a fierce level.

By testing her limits and tapping into her inner strength, Foreste shows us how to pursue our dreams. Her advice to aspiring Olympians? "Do all your homework: fitness, coaching, training, and psychological affirmations." And to her high school peers: "Don't be afraid of intense exams—show up prepared to brave *all* aspects of life."

POWER PRACTICE

Extreme sports like skydiving, bungee jumping, whitewater rafting, paragliding, and especially downhill skiing are physically and mentally very demanding and require a lot of courage. But many people—not just young competitors—try out these sports. What motivates them?

Mat Hoffman, BMX rider, famously explained, "If you want to experience all of the successes and pleasure in life, you have to be willing to accept all the pain and failure that comes with it." As mothers, we admire and salute all these courageous athletes and would like to add another quote, by Helmuth von Moltke: "First weigh the considerations, then take the risks."

TIPS ON HOW TO CREATE AN ATTITUDE OF COURAGEOUSNESS

How does an actress pluck up the courage to perform on stage? How do firefighters steel themselves to race into burning buildings? How does a recently widowed young mom find the strength to face each new day and keep going, despite her grief? How do any of us find the guts to ask for a raise, or a job promotion, or to ask someone new out for a date?

All of these acts require courage. But the truth is, for many of us, when we think of courage, we immediately think of our fears—fear of heights, cramped spaces, speaking up, facing risk. Many of us also think that attributes such as courageousness, bravery, and guts are qualities that others possess but are elusive to ourselves.

If you feel courage is elusive to you, do not fret. You are not alone. The good news is that experts are discovering that courageousness is a mind-set. According to a recent study on courageousness at West Point by lead author Lt. Col. Sean Hannah, we can actually reduce our level of fear when facing risk and create an attitude of courageousness, which can lead to future acts of courage.

The study (Hannah, Sweeney, Lester, 2007) found that

we can use affirmations and interpersonal emotional techniques to change our self-perceptions of courage, and that through that self-reflection we can create and reinforce our own courageous mind-sets.

Lt. Col. Hannah, the director of leadership and management programs at West Point, who teaches military personnel how to lead, says the research found that courage is driven by personality traits such as self-efficacy, hope, resilience, values, and beliefs, and by social forces. Even if we believe that we fall short on any of these personality traits, it is possible for all of us to tap into them and enhance them within ourselves.

Through this new model of courage, Hannah and his colleagues offer some ideas on the factors that feed into the subjective experience of courage. For example, he says that positive emotions are likely to lead to less experienced fear, which also leads to more courageous behaviors. For those of us seeking courage, Lt. Col. Hannah and his colleagues recommend that we work on building the following states of mind, which he calls "courageous states of mind":

- **Self-efficacy:** This involves affirmations and building confidence in ourselves by mastering a skill, like taking public speaking classes and seeing that we can build our confidence, or practicing speaking up to our bosses. Practice, practice, practice, Hannah recommends.

- **Creating hope:** We have to believe that something is possible and envision a way to make it happen. Hope can be increased through cognitive therapy, creating affirmations that positively show we can do something. "I am getting the job I want." "I am crossing the finish line at the marathon."
- **Building our resilience:** We all have experienced setbacks, or what we perceive as failures, but we have to develop our belief that we can overcome them. We have to practice the art of laughing off our fears and moving ahead after setbacks.

Lt. Col. Hannah and his colleagues identified the two most important factors needed for courage as our inner convictions and the social forces that surround us. "If deep within we believe in the power of selflessness and integrity and honor, these beliefs have important effects on us in the face of fear," he says. Also, courage is socially contagious. If we are looking for more courage in ourselves, we should look for role models in courage and emulate them.

CHAPTER TWO

TAKING THE FIRST STEPS TOWARD A COURAGEOUS MIND-SET

The opposite of courage in our society is not cowardice, it is conformity.

—Rollo May

Bravery does not have to be a spontaneous, split-second act of heroism—a bystander racing into a burning building to save a child, or an act of daring.

Often, courage can be found in the virtue and integrity of everyday acts—the mom who decides to seek treatment for her child's alcohol abuse, the laid-off executive who leaves his pride at home to wait tables to support his family, or the employee who speaks up about an injustice in the workplace.

Whether the opportunity to be courageous presents itself in routine action or in blazing a trail to leave a mark on history, courage gets its start when we see a way to carry it out. Often the first step on the road to empowerment is a baby step, when we make a decision to act in spite of our fear.

In our daily lives, we tend to create our own levels of comfort. One way to break these safety barriers is to take tiny steps outside our comfort zones and explore more of what life has to offer. These healthy challenges help us build our courage and reinforce our strength to keep acting courageously.

In this chapter, we introduce some wonderful courage guides who show us by example how to start off with small goals and changes to our lifestyles that can help inspire us to grow more courageous and forthright in our approach to the world.

Through their stories we find that when faced with something frightening, we can start simply by switching our thinking. Another lesson we learn from the people in this chapter is to surround yourself with people who will support you and help you believe in your skills and abilities. It's always much easier to try something new or something you fear if you've got a support team cheering you on.

These stories and the courage exercises you'll find throughout the book offer an outstretched hand to you as you take your first baby steps—or one huge jump—into that which scares you but will ultimately free you.

RANDOM ACTS OF COURAGE:
ORDINARY PEOPLE DOING
EXTRAORDINARILY BRAVE ACTS

It was a high counsel that I once heard given to a young person, "Always do what you are afraid to do."

—Ralph Waldo Emerson

When we think of bravery, we think of larger-than-life people who have made headlines and graced history books following their extraordinary acts of heroism and valor. Think Nelson Mandela or Martin Luther King. Or John F. Kennedy and Profiles in Courage, *Mother Teresa, Rosa Parks. These folk have reached super-human status for having the courage to defy the status quo, or they stood up for their beliefs in a revolutionary way. Some acted on behalf of others who did not have the courage to speak out for themselves.*

Sometimes we forget that despite their lauded status,

they too were ordinary human beings who made a choice to tap into their courage. And just like them, we all have the opportunity in our daily lives to make the world a better place or to stretch outside our comfort zones and do something revolutionary for ourselves.

It's easy to get hung up with the inner voice that says, Let's be real, I'm not Amelia Earhart. Or to pooh-pooh our own courage and limit our own behavior. "I'm a gutless wonder" becomes our mantra. Or "I've never been the brave type." As we researched this book, time and time again the people we reached out to told us: "Oh, I'm not courageous. I just did what I had to do." Or "I just did what anyone would do. No big deal."

We disagree. We believe that it takes guts to meet certain challenges of daily living and we applaud those who face their fears and don't take "no" for an answer. We consider these "random acts of courage." Our hope is that they will inspire you to move beyond your comfort zone and to know that you are not alone in the moments when daily life seems scary. All of us face challenges that make us shake in our boots. But we also believe that inside us lies the power to triumph over our fears and to tap into our brave hearts to create a life beyond our greatest expectations.

To help you kick-start your own inner gutsy girl (or guy), we took a closer look at the inspiring people we run into in our daily lives who remind us that challenges, big

and small, take a lot of courage. If they can do it, we can.
We hope you will be inspired too.

BLIND-SIGHTED

During the last several years, Mary Beth has made it her task to try to overcome her fears big and small, to lead a life that isn't spent tossing and turning in the wee hours of the morning, afraid of what lies ahead the following day. Even though she would like to think of herself as the little engine that could, there are days when the fear of raising three children on her own, facing the world after a recent job loss and having no clue what the future holds, makes her tremble.

She is so inspired every morning when she walks into the local YMCA to run or take spin classes and sees the elderly man swimming laps in the pool in the main lobby. Brady is blind. He swims back and forth along the rope, sometimes grasping it to make sure it is still there and that his stroke is on course.

It doesn't seem like a big deal, but Mary Beth has grown to consider this 80-something swimmer her courage guide. If he is not afraid of the occasional swallow of water, or the depths of a deep pool, if he can reach out grasping for a tether when he feels he panics and feels he's lost his direction, Mary Beth knows that she can leave the gym that day and be OK. Even if she chokes, or loses her path, she can tap into the inspiration of this older man who, despite his blindness, jumps into the pool every day and just keeps swimming ahead.

CHASING DREAMS

Another reminder of gutsiness for Mary Beth is the high school students at the inner-city Chicago school where she has helped some of the students surface their stories. These students, all African American, live in one of Chicago's most violent, gang-infested neighborhoods. Recently, a 14-year-old was shot and paralyzed blocks from the school, and there were five shootings in the neighborhood prior to that.

Most of these students have a story, and their stories would make many of us stay under the covers most mornings depressed and afraid to get out of bed. They've seen relatives shot in gang fights; many have never met their fathers or are being raised by a grandmother or a sibling. Poverty and the recession have ravaged their neighborhood, and they all know that bullets don't have eyes. Every day, en route to or from school, they fear a random bullet fired in a gang fight.

Yet they show up every day. They have big dreams. They have to have dreams, despite it all. Mostly, they have the courage to go after their dreams, despite odds that tell them dreams rarely come true. Most of these students come from single-parent homes, where college is only a dream and they are more likely to be arrested or killed than graduate from a university. They show up every day, dressed in shirts and ties and filled with hope that they can rise above the poverty and violence that surrounds them. They've got guts.

REAL RESILIENCY

Through our writing and volunteer work, we often come across people who are making a difference in the lives of others. Our journeys lead us to many fund-raising events. Nina recently attended a "Strictly Business" fund-raising luncheon put on by Jewish Vocational Services (www.jvs. org). She was brought to tears by the inspiring stories of the recipients of their "Employees of the Year" awards.

One who stood out was William Green. Raised by a single mother, William fell in with the wrong people when he was a teenager, and soon found himself looking at a 10-year jail sentence for bank robbery. In prison, wise words from an older inmate got him thinking, and William decided to turn his life around. He struggled after his release, living in a halfway house or on the street, but he was able to turn to the JVS Technology Access Center, the only place he had access to a computer to look for a job and a way out of his situation. With determination and the help of JVS, William landed a job at Deeelish Catering in San Francisco, where he is now the kitchen manager.

Olga Kashirtseva, a nurse who was forced to flee Russia to the United States with her children due to pervasive anti-Semitism, had to start her career over from scratch. She came to JVS and took advantage of everything they had to offer—vocational ESL taught her the language, office technology training helped her land her first American job, scholarships helped fund her training, and nursing refresher courses got her back into her nursing career. Today, Olga works as a registered nurse at Blood Centers of the Pacific in San Francisco.

Mary Beth recently attended the annual "Hope through Caring" dinner dance for the Les Turner ALS Foundation (www.lesturnerals.org) in Chicago. The ravages of this progressive neuromuscular disorder cause muscle weakness and impaired speaking, swallowing, and breathing, and it typically carries a death sentence two years after diagnosis. Those who live longer often live lives locked inside their own bodies.

Mary Beth was moved by the doctors and researchers at Northwestern University's Feinberg School of Medicine who in conversations beside the auction table described the patients whose resiliency, the fight to survive and thrive, they witnessed daily—people whose only hope is hope, hope that these folks in the laboratories will find a cure for this infliction.

She was moved by the family members of those who wage war with ALS and by people who have lost loved ones to it. And of course, moved by the patients, some who came from across the country—tethered to wheelchairs and fed in feeding tubes by their caregivers, decked out as if for the Oscars, who lovingly bring help and caring every day.

STAYING FEARLESS: THREE GENERATIONS OF FAMILY MEMBERS DISCOVER WHAT GUTSY MEANS IN THE FACE OF MEDICAL CRISIS

*Healing takes courage, and we all have courage,
even if we have to dig a little to find it.*

—Tori Amos

*"Is it courage? I'm not sure. We just did what needed to
be done, and continue to do so," Katey Merrill Foote says
as she describes the three and a half years since her granddaughter Ava was born. Ava was born with a medical condition that has left her blind and with the grim prognosis of
a shortened life expectancy. At three, the adorable little girl
with a Shirley Temple mop of curls and her own team of
supporters—Ava's Angels—has already defied the odds.*

*Leading the brigade is Katey, a grandmother of four
and mom of three grown daughters, including Ava's mom,
Lacey. It is her grown daughter, Katey insists, who has*

shown exceptional courage in the face of a situation that would be challenging to any and all of us.

Katey is the first to pooh-pooh any suggestion that the family's medical experience is courageous. She says she doesn't know how to be brave. But look close and you soon realize that this Iowa grandmother and her family hold the key to moving beyond the fear that can petrify or paralyze even the gutsiest of us.

If her story teaches us anything, it is that courage comes by taking action, and by moving ahead, one day at a time.

Katey Merrill Foote says she remembers the morning on August 3, 2007, when her daughter Lacey called and told her and her husband about their new granddaughter, Ava.

Lacey had a perfectly normal pregnancy in all respects. So her family and her medical team assumed everything would go as expected, just as it had when Hunter was born 20 months before. Katey recalls how she bought a new pair of running shoes for her daughter to help her take care of the rambunctious toddler Hunter.

When it was time for Ava to make her grand appearance, she did so with gusto. Her delivery took less than two hours. But immediately the anxiety alarms went off. Ava had a hard time breathing and was put in a tiny oxygen tent. Doctors diagnosed her with anophthalmia, the absence of eye tissue, and holoprosencephaly, meaning that her brain was not fully developed.

"I went into the shortest shock imaginable because I needed to stand firm and strong for her," Katey remembers. "When Lacey told me, I went into shock. I felt like I was in a bad dream that I couldn't wake up from. Numb. Unfeeling. Lost. Alone. I know this was a normal protective thing for my body. Ava's condition was a loss at the same time as it is a blessing, for she is still with us. She had trouble breathing for a while and that means we might have lost her right away without all the special care she is lucky enough to have."

In the days following Ava's birth, Katey started a website to garner support for Ava, Lacey, Lacey's husband, Scott, and the entire family. She wrote on the website: "Hi. I am Kate, and I have a granddaughter Ava who is struggling to live. She was born August 3rd, 2007, with no eyes. Her brain did not develop fully. We are dealing. We adore her, she is beautiful. She looks perfect. I welcome any support. I also would love to be there for any of you who need a shoulder and an ear."

During her three years, Ava has spent much of her life in and out of the hospital. At the same time, Katey has also struggled with her own health issues (a heart condition) and worrying about her aging father, who is 84 but still fairly independent.

Katey says that Ava and Lacey have taught *her* about bravery and fortitude. "Ava sees things none of us ever will. She hears what we sometimes neglect to appreciate.

She looks without judgment." Whatever the cause of what happened to Ava, "She is our little Ava Angel. She has been running the show from day one and we are at her service."

Katey says that Ava's other grandmother, Ann, described it best: "She said that God must think an awful lot of all of us, for he knew he could trust us to do the best for Ava. Bless you, Ann. We have so many caring people in our family. I know we will have all the support we need for the years to come. This is a long uphill road, but we travel it as a team."

Katey says that she often does not describe Ava's condition to others. "I hesitate to tell people about her eyes, for it is such a shocking condition and was so unexpected. Ava will not struggle with this issue, for she will not miss what she does not have. We as her family and friends will be the ones who have to deal with this."

Much of the family's support came from living at the Ronald McDonald House near the hospital where Ava was treated. "It helps to know that others are going through this sort of thing and that we can all help one another," Katey says.

She also says that she is inspired daily by her daughter Lacey and how she cares for Ava. "Lacey has always been a caring, compassionate person. She worked with special-needs people of all ages. She even worked in a nursing home and loved helping those wonderful older people. I think each person has courage. Some just get thrown into using it more than others."

Looking ahead, Katey says her wish for the future is "that people will understand that children with disabilities do not have a disease; children with disabilities are not looking for a cure, but for acceptance."

For now, Ava's future is in God's hands, as Katey and her family see it.

She says, "Just working on not thinking about the downside is my goal. I mourn for the part of life that Ava will never know. I hurt that she cannot run and play. I agonize when I see her brother [Hunter]'s love for her and know that odds are, she will leave him someday. He adores her. I am not sure if he connects that she should be able to play with him by this time or not.

"As for the rest of our families, I am so proud of Lacey's husband Scott's family—they stepped up immediately too. Not every family can do that, or will. And Lacey, she continues to be so strong. She rarely cries about it. She has little spells of letdown, and that is it. I don't know what happens when she is alone—I hurt thinking about that."

Katey continues, "As Ava gets older, it gets tougher, I am sure. There continue to be so many things to compare her condition to. I personally stopped doing that soon after she was born. We don't make a big deal of Ava's condition in public any more. It shocks people so much. If they do ask, we give a quick version. It is much harder on the people on the other side dealing with it than for us. We know no other Ava. We love her without question."

POWER PRACTICE

If you or a loved one are facing significant illness or a challenging medical situation, build your support network. Having a group of friends, family, and caring others to turn to for support can help you gather the courage to take each day at a time. Allow them to enfold you and your family with prayers, acts of kindness, and a listening ear.

FINDING COURAGE IN HEALTH CHALLENGES

Most people think of illness or health challenges as inconvenient at best, tragic at worst, according to Toni Weingarten, a San Francisco–area spiritual director and writer. Yes, illness is a time-out from our "normal" lives, but it needn't be time "lost." Certainly, illness gives us reason to be afraid, but by transforming this time into a spiritual practice, we find more strength to face it with bravery and courage.

Indeed, illness can be a fertile time if you can focus your attention away from what you do not have, and focus on what it offers in abundance. Even if your illness is one from which you may not recover, making it a spiritual practice will imbue your journey with rich rewards. To do this, we need to remind ourselves that spiritual practice is about bowing to and saying yes to the reality of life, even when that reality is illness.

"During my own pneumonia, my daily mantra and spiritual practice was the phrase 'It is what it is,'" Weingarten says. "When I came to fully embrace this concept, I felt a deep sense of peace with my situation. I gave in to my newfound understanding that my illness was as much a part of God's plan for me as my health. And I used my energy to heal instead of struggling against my unpleasant reality."

Toni Weingarten is a spiritual director with training in hospital chaplaincy. She lives near San Francisco and writes on faith, spirit, and religion. Visit her online at www.ToniWeingarten.com.

FORTITUDE IS HER FORTE:
FINDING PEACE AFTER CALAMITY

No one saves us but ourselves. No one can and no one may. We ourselves must walk the path.

—Buddha

In 1989, at the age of 31, Ruth Ann Liu-Johnston was driving on the upper deck of the Cypress Freeway in Oakland, California, during evening rush hour when the 7.1 magnitude Loma Prieta earthquake sent the upper deck crashing onto the lower deck. She remembers that she felt she lost control of her vehicle and was suddenly going way too fast. "I thought I was speeding, but I wasn't. I was airborne," she recalls.

Forty-one people were crushed to death in their cars, and Ruth Ann, after plummeting down to the lower deck, was trapped in a setting of carnage—and incredible courage. This experience, and a later brain surgery operation, put her on the front lines of fear management. Like so many others in the middle stages of their lives, Ruth Ann has experienced loss, pain, and fear, but it is her journey to understanding how the mind grapples with, and deals with, fear that defines her today.

A successful freelance graphic designer based in Oakland, Ruth Ann grew up in Vancouver, BC, and moved to the San Francisco Bay Area to attend California College of the Arts. She tells us about the terror—and heroism—of that day, and about the ways she has learned to cope.

"From the corner of my eye, I saw the guardrail snap—that's when I knew this was an earthquake," Ruth Ann Liu-Johnston remembers of that day when her car bucked and then plunged after the freeway collapsed.

She remained confined in her flattened automobile until two women—coworkers Lori Marsh and Lenora Moy, who also survived the fall in their car—pulled her out. Lori Marsh was injured, with two ruptured disks in her upper back, but she didn't realize it as she and Lenora went on to pull one man out of a truck leaking fuel and helped a man move a bloodied woman from underneath a truck. A particularly touching episode took place a few weeks later when the two women sent Ruth Ann's red high heels to her in the mail. She keeps them as a reminder of the courageousness of these two women.

"I've thought a lot about courage since that day," Ruth Ann muses. "I don't think it's an intended action, it's an action with intention. It is much more courageous to take conscious action in the face of danger than to simply react."

After hospitalization and extensive physical therapy, she recovered and kept very busy with her work and family. Nine years later, her stamina was again put to the test when she was diagnosed with Cushing's disease and underwent brain surgery to remove an adenoma tumor in her pituitary gland. She recalls being in a "gray space" between living and dying following her surgery. "After I was released from the hospital, I was in bed for three weeks," Ruth Ann recalls. "I remember that I didn't feel any fear about dying. For me, it took more strength and courage to make a commitment to stay alive."

"To deal with my stress and tension, I chant for a half hour each day and meditate the same amount of time," she says. She has always practiced Zen meditation, but two years ago discovered the Tibetan Nyingma Institute in Berkeley, California, whose motto is "Ancient wisdom for the modern world."

Head Lama and author Tarthang Tulku founded the Nyingma Institute in Berkeley in 1972 to present the teachings of the Tibetan tradition to the West. Over

150,000 students from throughout the world have participated in these programs, and the Nyingma Institute is recognized as a major center for Buddhist education in the West. Nyingma is the name of the oldest school of Tibetan Buddhism. Established in the 8th century, the Nyingma School has been a vital force in Tibet since that time.

Ruth Ann and her husband, Colin, completed a Buddhist psychology certificate program and are on the Nyingma two-year study program. Last year, they participated in a retreat on sacred sounds, and Ruth Ann completed a workshop on creativity based on the Nyingma Time/Space/Knowledge series.

"I credit this institute and its teachings with helping me to move beyond my fear," she said. "I originally turned to meditation to seek freedom from anxiety, but it continues to help me in so many different ways."

POWER PRACTICE:
Meditate. Meditation activates a deep source of inner peace that can protect us from suffering and frustration. Through sitting meditation, walking meditation, and mantra practice students at the Nyingma Institute learn to relax tension and cultivate equanimity. You can also learn how to reduce mental distractions by developing your own practice at home. There are many books and CDs available to help guide you through the process.

10 COURAGE RITUALS

Here are some things you can do when you are so scared that you question your ability to keep going.

First, think about being courageous for just this one moment, and then create your very own courage ritual. Here are some suggestions:

1. Create a safe place, an inner retreat in your imagination, and go there in your mind.

2. Extend loving support to yourself as you would to a good friend by looking in the mirror and repeating, "I love you."

3. Listen to soothing music.

4. Visualize yourself as a flower or a plant and imagine yourself getting nourished and basking in the sun.

5. Turn negative thoughts into positive ones and imagine a brand-new ending to your usual worries.

6. Cultivate an "attitude of gratitude" by giving thanks for your blessings.

7. Reach out to a trusted friend and ask to be nurtured.

8. Imagine yourself strong—visualize yourself as a superhero, or any other strong image.

9. Practice yoga stretches.

10. Consider adopting a pet.

CHAPTER THREE

OVERCOMING FEAR
AND FACING THE UNKNOWN

If you really don't believe that you can do something, you can say to yourself: I will turn pain into purpose. I will try to turn pain into a fulcrum that moves the world to help.

—ABC News anchor Diane Sawyer

We are living in difficult times. The stock market tumbles again. Headlines promise more waves of layoffs, more foreclosures, and a deeper recession. Businesses are closing. Swine flu and other health outbreaks threaten us on a seemingly daily basis. And headlines speak of global terrorists.

Who wouldn't have an anxiety attack just thinking about all this? How in the world are we supposed to act with courage in times fraught with so much talk of disaster? The great uncertainty of our time naturally provokes fear.

So how do we pursue our dreams at times when we so acutely face the fear of such huge unknowns? What do we do if we've lost our jobs? Or are thinking about changing a career, starting a new relationship, or making lifestyle changes? Our lives are fraught with experiences—large and small—where we must muster the courage to face the unknown.

One thing that the people featured in this chapter have shown us is that without personal courage, it is impossible to survive and thrive in times of great challenge. As poet Maya Angelou challenges: "You will face many defeats in your life, but never let yourself be defeated." That is the attitude the people in this chapter share—a willingness to meet life's challenges and to forge ahead in the unknown with the mantra "Never give up."

When we start to worry about the outcome, we can begin imagining awful things that aren't there. Worrying is not insurance that nothing will ever go wrong. Worrying doesn't substitute speculation for action; it is just an exhausting exercise. In this chapter we tell the stories of people who evaluated their options and harnessed their vivid imaginations to help them overcome fear.

It's also important to remember that you are not alone. Almost everybody worries about what will happen in the future. The prospect of not knowing whether something good or bad will happen to you in the near future can produce a lot of fear and anxiety. So, remember to take one day at a time. In this chapter, we look to role models who offer some specific steps for facing the fear of the unknown.

No one can predict the future or control what happens, but we can face our fears by preparing for the challenge. It's important to surround ourselves with support and to engage in positive self-talk or visualization of the outcome. Imagine yourself working in your dream job. We also can focus specifically on what it is we are afraid of and what is at stake and take appropriate action to make the change.

TOP 10 FEARS

1. Public speaking

2. Snakes

3. Confined spaces

4. Heights

5. Spiders

6. Tunnels and bridges

7. Crowds

8. Public transportation (especially airplanes)

9. Storms

10. Water (swimming and drowning)

(Source: Face Your Fears Today, www.faceyourfearstoday.com)

THE COURAGE TO CARE: WHEN HER HUSBAND WAS DIAGNOSED WITH MS, SHE HAD TO FIND STRENGTH AND COURAGE FOR TWO

Fear is the raw material from which courage is manufactured. Without it, we wouldn't even know what it means to be brave.

—Martha Beck

When a family member is diagnosed with a significant illness or chronic disease, the prescription for getting through what lies ahead typically involves strong doses of courage, strength, commitment, and love.

Suddenly, "normal" life is tossed on its head. That's exactly the experience Theresa Robbins had when her husband, Bill, was diagnosed with multiple sclerosis in June 2008. "Things are changing," she wrote in a news-letter she sent to her coaching clients on her website, www.theresarobbins.net.

Initially, she says, she went through "a period of intense freak-out for about two weeks when Bill was diagnosed—a period when I was just scared to death and living in absolute fear." But for the first two years, the progression of his disease was pretty slow and life did not change all that much. However, early in 2010 Theresa says it all changed. "I am thrust into a new reality," she wrote. "The symptoms he is experiencing indicate that his MS is progressing more rapidly than we had hoped. Since his diagnosis, I have not denied that his disease would progress and although I do believe in miracles, I have simply chosen to focus on what is happening right here, right now."

Through her experience, Theresa is in the process of launching a coaching support group for spouses of those who have received a devastating diagnosis. "I understand the fear and know my coaching skills are a huge help in dealing with my own stuff about my husband's disease," she says. "This allows me to get out of my own head and be more present in my life and in my marriage. Down the road, I imagine it will help me be a better caregiver. The coping, the fear management, keeps me in charge, not the disease. I want to offer that same kind of support for others because I get it."

Here she shares her journey to try to fight her inner fears—and keep them from spilling out and scaring her husband and children.

Two years ago, Theresa Robbins was a wife, a mother of two boys, and a life coach. Then a doctor's diagnosis changed everything. Her husband, Bill, was diagnosed with multiple sclerosis (MS) in 2008.

"Recently, my husband told me that he was experiencing an exacerbation," she says. Bill Robbins, a contractor who runs his own air conditioning and heating business, "is actually one of the most fearless and courageous people I have ever met," she says. "To those unfamiliar with MS, it is a disease in which the immune system attacks the nervous system. It destroys the myelin coating that acts as insulation for the nerves that carry electrical impulses throughout the body. When the myelin is destroyed, pain erupts, sensation is lost, and the ability to move and function normally deteriorates. An exacerbation indicates progression of the disease.

"As a trained coach, I know that circumstances do not make me feel anything. I control how I feel about circumstances by choosing my thoughts. I did not go into freak-out mode at the news of the exacerbation, but if I said I wasn't worried, I'd be lying. I make a conscious effort to be completely honest not just with other people, but with myself," she adds.

I immediately questioned Theresa about what she was thinking, because she says she knows her feelings come from her thoughts. "What I noticed was that I was projecting my fears into the future," she says. "I was feeling a little panicky because I was running all the possible negative scenarios through my mind. What does this mean for him? For me? For our family? I thought about the loss of his ability to do common everyday activities. I thought about how his inability to wrestle with the kids would affect them. I thought about having to care for our children, for him, for our home, for our finances, for everything on my own. I made it about what might happen, about what we might lose, about what I might lose."

Theresa has identified her fears as the output of what she calls "my lizard brain." She says, "It sounds pretty selfish. His MS is all about me, right? Well, that's what my lizard brain was thinking because it is designed to keep me safe, to protect me when threatened, and MS can definitely seem threatening. The problem is that sometimes my lizard brain runs amok imagining all sorts of crazy scenarios without me even really noticing that it's happening."

Theresa explains that the lizard brain is a part of our brain designed to keep us alive by alerting us to perceived threats. It is shaped like the brain of a reptile and is responsible for jolting us into "lack or attack mode." She says, "Lack mode comes from fearing that we don't have enough of something: time, money, chocolate, and so on. Attack mode comes when we imagine something horrible is going to happen. I was definitely feeling under attack and my lizard brain was not about to sit idly by and watch, so it sought to protect me by exploring all the horrible possible outcomes. The problem with this is that I stopped living here and now and started living in the perceived future."

Once she realized that her lizard brain was behind the fear, she felt a sense of relief. "It's just my lizard brain hard at work. So now what? I looked at how the fear is affecting me. I know that these fears paralyze me and prevent me from living joyfully, from living fully, from living authentically. They keep me locked in the selfishness and stop me from enjoying the time I have with my husband. This, by the way, is not how I want to live."

Recognizing that her thoughts were fueling the fear, Theresa decided to switch her thinking. "Instead of looking at what could happen, I chose to look at what *is* happening. And you know what? Right here, right now, everything is fine. My husband can still walk, tie his shoes, take a shower, and feed himself. Everything else was simply my imagination running away with me—I was projecting my fears into the future when I don't actually know what is going to happen in the future. If my projections are wrong, then I wasted a bunch of time wondering What if? And if they are right, well, so what? It's not like I gain anything by knowing I was right."

She sums up her attitude this way: "There is no reason to live today as though the future is here now. So I choose to enjoy today, appreciate what I have, and trust that I am capable of handling whatever comes my way."

POWER PRACTICE

Not all of us live with a loved one who has a debilitating disease, but at some point many of us have projected our fears into the future and starting living there instead of in the present. Theresa reminds us that it is important to keep focused on the present.

"Whether you have lost your job, lost your spouse, or have a kid who refuses to do their homework, if you worry about what it all means, you sacrifice your power to an imagined future," she says.

"Instead, examine the present. Today, in this moment, are you safe? Are you okay? If you are but feel fear anyway, you are probably projecting into the future and your own lizard brain is running the show," she says.

Just knowing that it is trying to keep you safe and that the future is nothing but your imagination, you can begin to put your fears to rest and live right here, right now.

DIVING INTO HOPE: DEAF AND BLIND, SHE INSPIRES OTHERS TO EXPLORE THE OCEAN'S REACHES AND THEIR OWN INNER DEPTHS

Nobody is born with courage. You have to develop courage the same way you do a muscle.

—Maya Angelou

When a genetic disorder stole her eyesight at 35, Ericka Remington, who was born deaf, vowed to help others break the barriers of their disabilities: "I am not a quitter" became her motto.

Now, 10 years later, this Jacksonville, Illinois, single mom of three has discovered scuba diving—and she is busy recruiting dozens of others with disabilities to the sport, to raise awareness and to create "a whole new world" of liberation and empowerment found in the realm beneath the sea.

"I was *really* scared, but I did it," Ericka Remington says.

On the eve of Ericka's elder son shipping out to Iraq, in July 2010, a foursome of strapping guys in wetsuits led Ericka across the sandy beach of Haigh Quarry, a scuba lover's paradise tucked amid the farmland in the eastern Illinois town of Kankakee and billed as "The Caribbean of the Midwest."

Wading about 10 yards into four-foot-deep water, Ericka's aquatic instructors started the drill: fins, scuba tanks, face masks, and instructions. The team that flanked her side was made up of a couple of Navy divers, an instructor trainer who dives the waters of the world from the Grand Caymans to Cozumel, and Remington's boyfriend, Rick Olsen, a blind military veteran who hand-signs with her, relaying her thoughts and feelings to the team. Underwater, he would communicate with the diver instructors via a full face mask with radio communications.

What bystanders may not have realized is that Ericka is blind and deaf. On that day, she was on a mission—for herself, for her three teenage children, for the community of blind and deaf people she trains in her town, and for others she inspires through a national organization for people with Usher syndrome, a relatively rare, incurable disease that robs its victims of hearing and sight.

She had come to the beach to break down a barrier for those like herself who face everyday life in the trenches of the world of physical disabilities and impairments, where freedom to navigate even the most mundane of tasks is often hard won. Remington was putting herself through a new challenge—diving into murky waters—to bring home a badge of courage and a message for her soldier son and for warriors with physical disabilities: "Fight for what you believe you can do. Never give up."

A couple of face masks and about a half hour into the training (her ponytail was just not cooperating), Ericka and her team disappeared under the murky waters, not to be seen for the next 45 minutes. She emerged triumphant. "I did it, I did it!" she relayed through her boyfriend, Rick. "I was *really* scared, but I did it."

Since then, she has spread the celebratory buzz and newfound love for scuba via e-mail to her circle of blind/deaf and deaf friends and mentees in the downstate Illinois town where she teaches Braille, and to the larger universe of folks she inspires to find the courage to see and experience the world through a different lens—their hearts and souls. Boyfriend Rick, who lost his eyesight in midlife, was a student. They bumped into each other—literally—at a picnic. "I knew I wanted to date her, but it took me a year of Braille lessons with her to be able to ask her," he says.

Now Ericka has rallied a group of others like her who will be trained in a weekend-long scuba diving program sponsored by Diveheart.org, a Downers Grove, Illinois–based nonprofit that helps wounded veterans—children and adults with disabilities who build confidence and independence through the adventure of scuba diving. To date, this group has guided more than 600 women and men like Remington on the adventure of scuba. In December 2009, Ericka and Rick traveled with the Diveheart group to scuba dive in Cozumel.

While many people think the world underwater is quiet and tranquil, Remington discovered on that steamy July afternoon that it is not only buzzing with activity, it brings her a freedom she has never experienced. Underwater, she is not inhibited by her disabilities; she can fly. She is hooked.

"My dream come true," Ericka says. "I always wanted to touch the bottom of the sea to feel shells and feel dolphins."

POWER PRACTICE
Just do it. Is there some adventure you always wanted to do in your life? Scuba dive? Ski? Ride your bike across the country? What are you waiting for? Sometimes, like Ericka, you have to dive into the murky waters, face your fears, and claim your triumph.

SPIRIT OF ADVENTURE AND A TRIP ACROSS THE WORLD: A LIFETIME OF LESSONS IN COURAGE

Only those who risk going far can possibly find out how far one can go.

—*T.S. Eliot*

It took guts to sell everything and move from California to Australia at the age of 22. But it took even more pluck and fortitude to stay. In this story, Ellen Goldstein recounts how her dream of sailing into the sunset took her on a journey to where she really belonged.

Now, years later, she knows that no matter what life throws in her path, she has a font of bravery to tap into whenever she needs to. Looking back, she has no regrets: "The courage I was able to summon when events took a sudden detour gave me experiences I will cherish forever, and helped me become the person I am today."

Through Ellen's story, we are reminded that finding our courage within is a gift, a well of wisdom we can dip into throughout our lifetime.

"I've been seeing someone else," he said.

This was not what Ellen Goldstein expected to hear, not after she had sold everything she owned and traveled halfway around the world on a one-way ticket to be with a sweet, smiling Australian shipbuilder she had known for only a few months.

Ellen and Peter met in San Francisco in 1971. On Christmas Eve, 1971, after a whirlwind courtship, Peter had to leave the country because his visa had expired. Ellen stayed behind for a few months to finish her last year of college. Their plans were to build a boat, sail around the world, and live happily ever after—an intoxicating dream that sustained her for the almost 8,000 miles to Sydney.

When the dream unraveled, Ellen thought about her options. Returning home was not one of them. "I had mustered my courage, sold my car and my treasured Fillmore posters and record albums. My parents were furious with me," Ellen recounts. "I decided that my life had brought me to this place for a reason, and even though I felt isolated and alone, I decided to stay to find out why."

When the full realization hit that Ellen's fate was in her own hands, and that she would have to chart her own path in this distant land, she took long, solitary walks on the beach to try to figure out how to calm her fears and tap into her inner strength.

She soon found work in a camera shop in Sydney's red light district, which required an hour-and-a-half drive or ferry ride from the North Shore, where she lived with Peter.

"Eventually I made friends with an American girl who was working for a Meher Baba company, Don't Worry Be Happy, and she got me a job there. It was a fun place to work," Ellen remembers.

While she was working there, several of her photos were made into posters—one of a monkey smoking a cigar and another of a monkey reading a newspaper—and were huge sellers. She also taught photography and sold macramé wall hangings in local shops. "Peter broke it off with the girlfriend and we began to rebuild our relationship," she says. On the weekends, she helped him build his boat, although she doubted that she would ever set foot on its deck.

For two years she saved up money to explore as much of Australia as she could before returning to America. "For four months, I hitchhiked around the continent, encountered fellow travelers, and had the experience of a lifetime," Ellen says. "Although I was apprehensive about going alone, I came to relish the opportunity, as well as the feeling of being footloose and unfettered for probably the one and only time in my life."

"On my journey, I stripped sugarcane in Queensland until my hands bled, and caught rides with a variety of interesting, and occasionally unsavory, characters. A fishing charter on the Great Barrier Reef took me on as a cook and bottle washer for a week."

Eventually she landed in Darwin—two weeks before it was nearly destroyed by a tsunami. It was there that Ellen hooked up with a family of five on a similar odyssey over the remote unpaved roads of Western Australia. "We had a very special connection and are still in touch today."

She reminisces: "We swam with sharks on the Eighty-Mile Beach, saw a fast-moving object in the night sky that could only have been a UFO, hiked naked down the imposing Katherine Gorge, and showered under a spigot at an outback cattle station. It was a marvelous adventure, and I took a ton of photographs, most of which unfortunately were damaged in the heat of Australia's outback, although a few survived."

When she returned from her travels, Peter seemed to have a newly developed appreciation for her and her newfound fearlessness. He wanted to get married and carry out the dream. But for Ellen, the smiling, carefree Aussie she had met in San Francisco had become a moody, negative person with a chip on his shoulder. And she had changed as well.

"The baggage he had left behind when I met him in America was all too present in his native land," she says, "and I realized that we had sort of changed places—I had left all my baggage behind, and wasn't terribly interested in being saddled with his."

They continued to live together and work on the boat, but she knew deep down that the dream that had brought them together was not going to happen. Soon she began to feel isolated, rarely speaking to her family back in San Francisco—at $25 a call it was too expensive, and they almost never called her.

Things reached a tipping point when she received a letter from her brother describing all the things that were happening back home. The streaking fad was in full swing, there were free concerts in Golden Gate Park, and he and his friends were sliding down the fairways at Harding Park Golf Course on blocks of ice. "I realized that San Francisco was my home, I had to get back," she says.

Fortunately, she was able to save enough money for the ticket home as she and Peter continued to work on the boat. She let Peter know she was returning to San Francisco one week before he planned to put the boat in the water, and she surprised her family by arriving, three years to the day, on Christmas Eve, 1974.

"I never looked back," Ellen says. "I don't know what happened to Peter or his boat, but I felt that my experience in Australia had given me the life experience I had come for, and that the leap of faith I had taken to pull up stakes and go to the other side of the world had paid off in unexpected ways. The courage I was able to summon when events took a sudden detour gave me experiences I will cherish forever, and helped me become the person I am today."

These days, Ellen co-owns Bullseye Creative Services in San Rafael, California, with her husband, Dan Reich. Together they provide photography, graphic, and Web design and other creative services for businesses, nonprofits, and start-ups.

POWER PRACTICE

We empathize with those who feel their lives are in limbo for any number of reasons. It is much easier to live with the certainty and security of the known. Yet even with all our planning, we can never predict everything that will happen. Answers are not always at our fingertips.

When experiencing dread of the unknown, it helps to remind ourselves that even though right now we don't know how things are going to turn out, we can honor the present, and eventually, the answers will present themselves.

DOWNWARD MOBILITY: HARD LESSONS DURING RECESSION LEAD TO RESOURCEFUL NEW DIRECTIONS

This is no time for ease and comfort. It is the time to dare and endure.

—*Winston Churchill*

Like most of us, Marlene Baroli-Turati thought she would be prepared for fluctuations in her lifestyle and felt that she could handle them. But as the Lake Forest, California, single mom of two daughters discovered, nothing quite prepares you to handle the blow of being laid off—and meet the challenge of keeping your dignity intact too.

Finding out you have lost your job is one of those life challenges that can become overwhelming, completely deflating our self-esteem and destroying our sense of worth. Not to mention feeling scary, personally and financially.

As Marlene discovered when she lost her management post at a Fortune 500 company, taking the first step after losing your job requires a lot of faith and fortitude. Here, she shares how she put on a brave face and continued to forge ahead, despite the sudden loss of her professional identity, including her income, her routine, and the camaraderie with her coworkers. Struggling to keep feelings of failure at bay, there were times she wanted to cry like a child.

In 2008, after working 20 years at her company, Marlene Baroli-Turati, 44, lost her job as Creative Services project manager for the Southern California division of the Boeing Company. She was making $94,000 a year plus a company matching 401k, health insurance coverage, paid education, a virtual office, paid cell phone, and a laptop computer, to name some of the perks.

Since then, Marlene has done everything from babysitting and secretarial work to cleaning houses. Although she has a master's in business administration and is trying to make the best of her situation, it has been hard. She says, "I had car loans, college loans, a mortgage, and a certain level of lifestyle that included my kids being in club soccer, private colleges, travel, and an active social life. Our lifestyle was built around my salary. My teenager got a new car for her birthday and we did mom-daughter trips to the mall. We lived a very comfortable middle-class life."

"I found it very difficult to survive, and it was impossible to get a job to replace my income," she recalls. "After three months I had to do what I had to do to pay my bills—I applied to any and every job I could, from Walmart to every store at the mall."

Soon afterward, the family of three moved from their 4,000-square-foot, six-bedroom home to a much smaller dwelling, and Marlene is renting their former home to pay the mortgage and save it from foreclosure.

"We sold everything we did not need, excess furniture, drum set, bikes, etcetera," she says. "We also gave up everything that was not really necessary to survival, such as soccer and Girl Scouts, and our social life changed dramatically as well. No more movies, no more dinners, no more trips to Disneyland."

The priorities became simple: pay mortgage, pay rent, pay utilities, pay car insurance, and eat. "If it didn't fit those categories, we didn't do it. This is a concept that has been life-altering and hard for my girls."

The Orange County resident's lowest moment came, she says, when she was cleaning houses. But she also credits the epiphany with catapulting her into facing her fears and pushing herself completely out of the box.

At first she thought the family's situation would be temporary. "I am a professional, have skills and talent, and would find a job, not necessarily the same job, but any office would hire me," she says she remembers thinking.

"I thought in three months I would have a salary and things would go back to normal, but months went by, and nothing." She had accumulated dozens of variations of her résumé. When the holidays arrived, she applied at every store in four malls. But still, nothing.

A year ago, she launched her own business. As she tells it, "The most challenging moment was the day I cleaned the home of two young ladies who appeared to have *never* cleaned their place. I spent six hours scrubbing the bathtub, toilet, and kitchen, all for forty dollars! I decided then and there that I had to take matters into my own hand, and started my own business."

She started selling her homemade jam to local shops and online. You can find her delicious products at www.etsy.com/shop/dasweetzpot.

Since then, she has expanded her strategy and her product line and is focusing all her time on the business. And it's taking off. It still does not pay all her bills, but she believes she is moving in the right direction.

"It has been an emotional roller coaster," she says. "I did not lose my job because I was incapable or irresponsible. I almost had to foreclose my home, and not because I was financially irresponsible either. I have paid all my bills, and tried everything I could to make it on my own. At times it seemed like the end of the world. It was the end of the world as we knew it."

But she is focusing on the positives. "I learned to be

strong. I learned I could get through it and do whatever I had to do to protect my family."

Five Tips for Managing Your Fears after Job Loss
Marlene offers these tips:

1. Explain to your children how a parent losing their job will affect them. They do not need to understand the financial aspect (depending on their age, it is hard to explain), but they need to know that their lives will be affected by the loss of job. It is nothing to be ashamed of.

2. Don't worry about what your friends think or say. The fact of the matter is, nobody knows what you are going through unless they went through the experience themselves. Try to surround yourself with positive people who will make you feel good, because you are already in a bad place emotionally.

3. Don't be embarrassed to explain to your friends that your spending priorities have changed, and although you wish to remain friends and maintain the social life you had

(trips, spa, and girls' night out), you really don't have the cash to be able to spend to keep up with them. It is OK to host potlucks at home. It is the friendship that counts, not the things you do with your friends. Those who don't understand, let them move along; they are not truly your friends.

4. Tap into your other skills and talents.

5. Pay it forward. If you can help someone along the way, help them. It will come back in some way, shape, or form. Someone can learn from your experience.

GETTING HELP WITH IDENTIFYING
THE SOURCE OF YOUR FEARS

Many people turn to professional help to cope with specific fears, such as phobias (fear of flying or heights) or social anxieties (fear of public speaking or leaving the house). However, fear is often an underlying issue in many common problems, such as work stress, marital conflict, low self-esteem, and life transitions. It also contributes to symptoms of depression, anxiety, eating disorders, and sleep problems, which in severe cases can have debilitating effects if not treated. When people can identify, acknowledge, and accept their fear, they have more choice in how to respond to fearful events or situations, instead of unconsciously reacting out of their fears.

Michele Kirk, a marriage and family therapist in private practice in the San Francisco Bay Area, helps clients work through their fears in a variety of ways.

Here is her advice on how to work with fears that keep us stuck. The first step is to identify a specific fear (social anxiety), and understand its connection to unpleasant feelings (feeling scared, cautious, shy), physical symptoms (increased heart rate, stomachache), and unwanted behaviors (drinking, sleeping). Michele then helps clients address each of these factors. Clients learn healthy coping skills, such as relaxation and self-care, for dealing with uncomfortable emotions, and this in turn decreases physical symptoms. Clients also learn to reduce stress in their lives and utilize social supports, instead of turning to destructive habits.

The deeper work is helping clients identify automatic thoughts (Nobody likes me, I am unlovable) that feed the anxiety and fear and keep them stuck. Michele teaches clients how to challenge those thoughts by looking for evidence against them (I have many friends, people frequently invite me to social events) and considering alternative hypotheses. Clients are then able to replace negative self-thoughts with more positive and realistic thoughts (I am lovable and deserving of love), which leads to improved mood and positive behavior change as well.

You can visit Michele at www.michelekirk.com.

CHAPTER FOUR

THE COURAGE TO BEAR WITNESS TO SPEAK OUT

Courage is contagious. When a brave man takes a stand, the spines of others are often stiffened.

—Billy Graham

Most of us don't set out to become an activist in our own lives—or to call out our differences. In fact, we're taught from an early age to do anything but differentiate ourselves: "Be a good boy." "Don't rock the boat." "There's strength in numbers."

We've heard them all, and we're sure you probably have too.

Except that sometimes we stand at pivotal moments in our own lives and the lives of others. We can do nothing—make sure we still fit in, and not make metaphorical waves. It's easier sometimes to stay silent. But then we must watch as wrongs continue; families are torn apart by dysfunction; corporate leaders make unethical choices; someone we know is struggling; or there are homeless people in our communities desperate for something to eat or a place to sleep. We can stay silent, or we can stretch outside our comfort zone to stand with those who need us.

If there is a chapter in this book that speaks most profoundly to the personal experience of both of us, it is probably this one. In our lives we have had to make tough choices that required us to challenge ideas and stand up to intimidation. We've both experienced profound dread and anxiety and cataclysmic personal catastrophes.

We know what it feels like to be threatened and to be frightened of an unknown future. But we also know that when you are willing to take a stand, when a stand needs to be taken, you are showing yourself—and the world— that you have the courage to take control of your life and take it to another level, to strive for what is better and what is right.

It's not easy. Courage is a risky business. But all of us have inside us principles and beliefs that define who we are and what we stand for. Our values make us different from everyone else. When we compromise these basic ideals we are not really living, and often the result is much confusion and unhappiness—or worse, we watch our dreams and aspirations fade away, or get stomped on by someone else.

In this chapter, we take a look at the lives of several

people who we believe are especially brave for the way they have drawn a line in the sand and taken a firm stand for what they believe. It's not always easy. But it is always right.

THE WOUNDED HEALER: DOMESTIC VIOLENCE TURNED INTO A MISSION TO CLAIM POWER AGAINST ABUSERS

Ultimately we know deeply that the other side of fear is a freedom.

—Marilyn Ferguson

Scared, alone, and feeling broken, Alexis A. Moore called her local domestic violence center. She was battered and beaten. The year was 2004. She was 30 years old and had spent the previous six years on a relentless roller coaster of emotional and physical abuse.

But it was the fear that froze her and prevented her from taking action that scared her most.

When she finally sought help, it became clear why she was so afraid and why it took her so long to find the strength to leave: the intensity of her ex-boyfriend's rage was terrifying. He embarked on a campaign of what is known today as "cyberstalking"—using technology to harass, terrify, and control Alexis on a daily basis. He did not stop there.

Here, Alexis bravely shares the story of how she found the courage to fight for and claim her freedom. In the process she finally found something to hope for. And the good news is, she turned her own pain and very frightening experience into a learning experience to help other victims of abuse and crimes, from identity theft and elder abuse to rape and sexual assault.

Alexis Moore was living in El Dorado Hills, California, and dating a high-tech investigator/information broker. At first, things seemed fine. But soon, his controlling behavior and emotional insults, which evidently in his mind were not enough to obtain the power and control he coveted, escalated into physical threats and actual physical violence.

In November 2004, a brutal beating left Alexis with permanent nerve damage and the determination to leave. Or to try to escape. "Leaving this person physically did not help me escape the threats to my well-being," she recalls. Even from a distance, his abuse and his controlling behavior continued.

"He was able to change my mailing address so that I stopped receiving mail from my bank, credit card, and insurance companies," she says. "He accessed my cell phone records so he was able to see who I was calling and also infiltrated my mother and grandmother's phone records."

His campaign of terror became even more menacing with each day. "He began to cancel my credit cards and insurance and also electronically transferred funds from my accounts so that I would be overdrawn by the time I discovered it," she says.

When Alexis reached out for help from local and state law enforcement agencies she was told that it was a civil matter and that these activities were not criminal. That is when she began her journey to challenge the legal system. "It was not easy, to say the least," she remembers. "I was essentially homeless, floating between my relatives' homes, and I had no money and only the clothes that I had on my back for several months. I was in severe pain from the beatings."

She spent hours each day contacting credit card companies, banks, her auto insurance carrier, and her medical health insurance provider, trying to get someone to understand that she was experiencing cyberstalking *not* identity theft—because he was not stealing money; he was using her identity to harass and control her from afar.

But in those darkest days and weeks, Alexis found a core courage and strength. She learned how to corral her panic to transform her fear into action. She set forth on a mission to document her tormentor's stalking crimes by faxing letters, closing bank accounts, and showing the evidence to law enforcement officers, her attorney, and the FBI—"whoever would listen to me if only for a second to let them see what was happening." Most dismissed her as a hysterical female seeking revenge from a scorned ex.

Two years into the process, in January 2006, she met her current boyfriend, who helped her escape the serious emotional damage and further overcome her fear to lead a full and abundant life. Under his tutelage, she practiced and trained for situations where her safety and well-being might be compromised.

"When I am feeling threatened today," she explains, "after an unexpected knock at the door or a suspicious car drives by or appears to be following me, rather than becoming paralyzed with fear, I do what I have practiced doing, and that comfort zone kicks in."

Having faced her deepest fears head-on, Alexis has powerful advice for other women seeking the courage to confront their own demons.

She offers these five tips for facing and overcoming fear:

1. CREATE A FEAR MANTRA. Turn fear into a positive by reminding yourself, even out loud, that you are in control of your own feelings.

2. JUST BREATHE. Control your breathing by reminding yourself to take a breath.

3. SEEK SUPPORT. Speak with persons you know will be understanding, who will be able to listen if you need to talk. If a friend is going through a stressful divorce or losing her job, she is probably not the right choice of someone to speak to regarding a fearful situation that you are going through.

4. SEEK THE COUNSEL OF TRUSTED EXPERTS. Consult trusted professionals—a priest, pastor, counselor, teacher, or someone else capable of being objective and not imposing their own views and opinions on your actions.

5. WRITE YOUR FEELINGS. Express your feelings in a journal. This will help you release them instead of keeping them bottled up inside.

Today, Alexis is a go-to person internationally for issues pertaining to domestic abuse, stalking, privacy protection, and credit collections, as well as the new phenomenon of cyberstalking. Under Alexis's leadership, the group Survivors in Action is spearheading a movement known as

DV Reform, which exposes the harsh realities faced by victims of domestic violence and abuse throughout the nation and is working to help garner the support of the newly appointed White House advisor for violence against women, Lynn Rosenthal.

Looking back, Alexis says the experience has helped her redefine her sense of self and has empowered her to be much more than she ever imagined.

"This experience made me a very strong leader and a powerful speaker and writer, which I never thought I was," she reflects. "It helped me to try new things like yoga that I had never experienced before. And it provided me with a stronger, more grounded foundation that helps me to appreciate my everyday life—smelling the fresh-cut grass or just sitting and watching children play or accomplishing a workout at the gym are far more special now. I love and live better now than I ever have before, and it is all because of this experience that some say was a horrible ordeal. I say it was the best thing that could have happened to me."

POWER PRACTICE

I realized that fear was not helping me, it paralyzed me. In fact, it kept me from achieving success overall and from reacting the way I needed to under pressure. So I turned the fear into anger and often into laughter. When I was fearful for my safety or for the safety of those around me, I would remember that it was up to me to stay calm, and I talked to myself—out loud and often. I still do to this day. I remind myself that fear is something that is in my realm to embrace or make go away all by myself.

—Alexis A. Moore

TAKING ON THE BOYS' CLUB: PUSHING PAST FEAR TO STAND BY HER VALUES

Most of our obstacles would melt away if, instead of cowering before them, we should make up our minds to walk boldly through them.

—Orison Swett Marden

Have you ever been in a situation where someone told an offensive joke and everyone around laughed? Did you walk away wishing you had said something, anything? In this story, Ann Mehl takes on an entire corporate culture and shows that standing up to address a toxic situation— even at the risk of her job—is no laughing matter.

We applaud the guts it took to stand up to her colleagues and peers to right a wrong. It is not a moment that most of us would come easily to.

* * *

Ann Mehl started her first job in 1995 at a boutique firm that specialized in staffing technology talent for Fortune 500 companies and innovative start-ups. "It was during the dot-com boom and young firms that placed technology candidates were growing like wildfire," she says. "It was a bit of the Wild West in my office."

"The company hired recent college grads, and I was one of the few females on the floor, which was an open pit." (Think of the movie *Boiler Room*.) "We were all on a hundred-percent commission-based salary, in terms of the pay structure. If you made a placement, you'd ring a bell that was mounted in the middle of the office and then high-five everyone. With this showboating and salesy environment came macho attitudes and brazen egos."

As the Internet fever grew, so did the online porn industry, and the men in her office became "daily inspectors of anything bold and outrageous when it came to XXX sites," as Ann puts it.

"Soon it became apparent that pictures were being viewed and downloaded during office hours and the lack of professional management created a cavelike atmosphere," Ann recounts. "The boys were viewing and sending pictures to one another constantly and calling each other over to their desks to check out the latest obscene photos. As part of my job responsibilities I interviewed clients in our office, and I often found that the guys left their computers

94

on with the porn shots still open on the screens."

Ann remembers that there was so much of this happening on a regular basis that she often found herself upset and offended, especially as it became more rampant. During one of the weekly staff meetings, she finally got up the courage to say something. In front of the CEO and the entire company she stood up and expressed her disappointment at the behavior.

"I was shaking, as I hadn't practiced what I was going to say, but I kept going," she recalls. "I said that downloading porn during office hours was completely unacceptable and I wanted it to stop immediately. One of the wiseacres in the office laughed out loud and said, 'What constitutes business hours?' "

She didn't back down. She replied, "Any hour that I am here in the office, and beyond that—any time our company doors are open." She described the incidents when she found herself uncomfortable while porn photos were being shared and left up on the work monitors.

As she recalls, "I added that I was sure that EEOC law would dictate that the firm was liable for the unprofessional behavior if they noted what was going on. Then I sat down. One person started to clap and the founder of the firm, likely afraid of a pending lawsuit, said, 'Ann, you are absolutely correct and it has to stop.' "

Today, Ann Mehl lives in New York and is a certified coach through the Life Purpose Institute and Martha

Beck's NorthStar program. You can learn more about her at her website: www.annmehl.com.

Her experience with the boys' club remains in her memory. "I didn't find it easy to speak up, and even though I was a bundle of nerves, I thought to myself, I am so proud of you. No matter what transpires, someday you'll tell your daughter about this and you'll be happy that you stood up for yourself."

POWER PRACTICE

If you want to speak up to right a wrong, but feel intimidated, even terrified, it helps to remind yourself that many people do courageous things when they are scared stiff.

If your emotions are keeping you from doing what you know you must, think about courage as something that you need to "do" even though you don't feel like it. You don't need to get to the source of your fears and alleviate your fears all at once. You can simply tell yourself that just this time, despite your feelings, you're going to put on a cloak of courage and "just go for it."

A BRAVE DOZEN:
GOING OUT ON A LIMB FOR THEIR BELIEFS

The image of "going out on a limb" conjures someone crawling to the end of a tree limb and hanging on for dear life. One wrong move and the limb may break and crash.

In real life, there are folks who have put themselves in harm's way to stand up for what they believe in: people who have reached far beyond the safety of the tree trunk in order to make a difference. Many times, these people do so in spite of harsh criticism.

This is the essence of the expression "to have the courage of one's convictions." Gutsy people throughout history—both famous and unknown—epitomize that trait.

Here are just a few recent examples, from around the world, of people who went out on a limb to express their convictions, even at the risk of scrutiny and censure. Whether our beliefs jibe with theirs or not, we honor their bravery and courage.

1. It took a lot more than "Three Cups of Tea" to find his courage, but Greg Mortenson put his life at risk to build schools in small villages in Afghanistan and Pakistan. He

had a fatwa issued against him because he was trying to promote girls' education.

2. Human rights defender Rita Mahato has been threatened with rape, kidnapping, and death as a result of her work helping women in Nepal who have suffered acts of violence. She is a health adviser at the Women's Rehabilitation Center, which has been attacked by men from the village who object to WOREC's work.

3. Daniel Choi, an American infantry officer in the United States Army, served in combat in the Iraq war during 2006–2007. He became an activist after coming out as a gay man on *The Rachel Maddow Show* in March 2009, and in March 2010 he and fellow soldier James Pietrangelo chained themselves to the front gate of the White House in protest of the US military's "Don't Ask, Don't Tell" policy, which forbids lesbian, bisexual, and gay service members from serving openly.

4. Julia Bonds, a coal miner's daughter and the director of Coal River Mountain

Watch in West Virginia, is a community leader against the practice of mountaintop removal that is steadily ravaging the Appalachian mountain range and forcing many to abandon their homes.

5. In 1955, Nawal El Saadawi graduated from the University of Cairo with a degree in psychiatry. In 1972, she lost her job in the Egyptian Ministry of Health because her book *Women and Sex*, published in Arabic and banned by the political and religious authorities, spoke up against female genital mutilation. In 1981, she was arrested and imprisoned along with other Egyptian intellectuals under Anwar Sadat's regime. She was released upon Sadat's death in 1982, and shortly thereafter founded the Arab Women's Solidarity Association (AWSA), an international organization dedicated to "lifting the veil from the mind" of Arab women.

6. Jack Kevorkian became known as "Dr. Death" for his work assisting many people in committing suicide. Kevorkian considered the right to die to be a basic

personal right, having nothing to do with government laws. He felt there could be a time when a suffering person may choose death and that physicians should be allowed to assist. In 1997, however, the US Supreme Court ruled that Americans who want to kill themselves—but are physically unable to do so—have no constitutional right to end their lives. Kevorkian was sentenced to 10–25 years in prison, and was paroled in 2007.

7. Cindy Sheehan, an antiwar activist whose son, Specialist Casey Sheehan, was killed during his service in the Iraq War in 2004, attracted national and international media attention for her extended antiwar protest at a makeshift camp outside President George W. Bush's Texas ranch.

8. Daw Aung San Suu Kyi, the Nobel Peace Prize laureate in Myanmar, the nation formerly known as Burma, co-founded a pro-democracy political party that sought to counter the military junta that had reigned over that country since 1962. For 14 of the past 20 years, Aung San Suu Kyi

has endured unofficial detention, house arrest, and restrictions on her movement. She continues to be held under house arrest in Yangon.

9. Journalist Anna Politkovskaya reported about the human rights situation in the Chechen Republic for the newspaper *Novaya Gazeta*. She had also written extensively about abuses in other parts of Russia, such as violence in the army, corruption in state structures, and police brutality. She was detained, threatened, and poisoned because of her work. In October 2006, she was shot dead at her home in Moscow.

10. Julia Butterfly Hill literally went out on a limb for two years when she moved into a 1,500-year-old California Coast Redwood tree she named "Luna." Her 738-day protest was intended to send a strong message to loggers of the Pacific Lumber Company not to cut "Luna" down.

11. Women of Zimbabwe Arise (WOZA) organized peaceful demonstrations to protest the worsening social, economic, and human

rights situation in Zimbabwe. They have been repeatedly harassed, intimidated, beaten, and jailed by authorities.

12. Ingrid Newkirk is president and co-founder of People for the Ethical Treatment of Animals (PETA), the world's largest animal rights organization. She has been criticized for her support of actions carried out in the name of the Animal Liberation Front. Her position is that the animal rights movement is an extreme one, and that "thinkers may prepare revolutions, but bandits must carry them out."

TAKING A STAND FOR THE OPPRESSED: HE FOLLOWS HIS DREAM TO A NEW LIFE

Security is mostly a superstition. It does not exist in nature ... Life is either a daring adventure or nothing.

—Helen Keller

In December 2009, Hans Hageman, 52, left a six-figure executive director job at a major New York nonprofit. Although the school's mission is to bring hope to high school students who might otherwise not have any, Hans resigned because he says he believed that the organization's mission was taking second place to its financial struggles. He says he felt executive board decisions were compromising the best interests and long-term goals of preparing the high school students for college and careers beyond. "I became concerned about how we were losing focus on the teens we needed to be serving. We had lost touch of our purpose and I could not justify the hypoc-risy, so I resigned," he says.

Though fiercely committed to organizations dedicated to improving the education and health of disadvantaged children and their families, Hans is reinventing the route he is taking to help educate and support teens in need.

The leap has been an especially daring and scary one. Hans had previously navigated the transition from presti-gious positions as a government and corporate attorney to forge a career launching nonprofits and making a differ-ence in the lives of teens in New York, India, and Africa. Now, in standing up against what he believed smacked in the face of his intentions, he felt severed from his goals, and his family faced financial challenges.

Hans and his wife, Bernadette, are the parents and adoptive parents of 10 children ages three through 27. (Both were married previously and have combined their families.) And they are helping to support several other teenagers in need, including a student from Senegal who lives with the family in their renovated East Harlem brownstone.

Growing up in New York, Hans Hageman and his two siblings lived above an experimental drug rehabilitation center, Exodus House in Harlem, which housed and coun-seled recovering drug addicts, mostly Vietnam veterans. It was founded by their parents, Lynn (a Methodist minister) and Leola, an African American Chicago native and community activist. "My parents were fearless," he remembers. "They just did what they believed needed to be done to help others."

These early lessons propelled him. Hans grew up passionate about making a difference in the lives of those on the margins. He graduated from Princeton and then Columbia University School of Law. He was a rising star: Hans served on the Senate Judiciary Committee for the Constitution, as a narcotics prosecutor in his role as chief counsel for the New York City District Attorney's office, and as an attorney for a prestigious corporate firm.

But it was not enough. He wanted to reach back to his parents' simple but stirring commitment to help the less fortunate. In his role in the New York City court system he met a fellow state's attorney, John Kennedy Jr., who later helped him and his brother found a high school for at-risk students in Spanish Harlem. "Being able to face the unknown and the unbridled fear that is part of the world today is to be as flexible as you can and to be always evolving," Hans says.

In the years that followed, Hans was invited to India, where he visited several poor villages. There he met hundreds of out-of-school children, especially girls, and witnessed the absolute poverty (families with earnings of less than $1 per day.) In spite of the size and scope of the problem, Hans felt compelled to do something to improve the lives of the children he met. Upon returning to New

York, Hans donated his savings to open the Sulaxmi School for Girls in August 2002 to educate girls in the villages of Gomti Nagar, in Lucknow, India.

The next year, the couple founded the Salus Foundation to provide financial support to the Sulaxmi School for Girls and other programs dedicated to improving the education and health of disadvantaged children and their families. Hans and his wife continue to run this foundation today. In the midst of that commitment, the family stayed centered on the families in the Harlem district of New York City, where Hans had been raised. There, he helped found two high schools and pledged his passions.

Many good things were set in place at the schools, and the goals seemed right, but the mode of operation was not, so late last year Hans had to make a tough choice and walk away.

Reinventing himself again, he is tapping into his other skills as he reenvisions how he can make a difference. Among other things, he is a Reiki master, a certified sports performance coach, and a Level 1 boxing coach, and he trains police departments in interview and interrogation techniques. He is putting these skills to use as an educator and trainer and coach for teens and baby boomers—he is a "transformational coach," which Hans says "causes some of my fellow alums from Princeton and Columbia University to react as if I have two heads."

"My family and I are living a very frugal life—no cars,

no vacations, and no really expensive things," Hans says. "But we are rolling out a new way of doing what we are committed to doing, and doing it with character. Yes, there has been a price to pay, but we will find our way and do what we are meant to do, the right way."

He continues: "In my opinion, people need to be clear about their values; otherwise life just seems to happen. Freedom and service rank high for me. I believe we all have a special gift to share with the world and part of my definition of hell is not allowing yourself to detect this gift. For those of us who have children, what lessons do we want them to take from our lives?

"It's okay to be scared, but you can either freeze or act anyway. I often take inventory of the things that are going right in my life, and this provides fuel. World events have shown that change is the only given and adaptability and flexibility can be learned. Social media offer good tools for facilitating this. Knowing when to quit is another important skill I've learned. I also have an abiding faith."

POWER PRACTICE
Tips for finding the courage to take a stand, recommended by Hans:

1. Develop a meditation/prayer practice for stress management and to practice being in the present.

2. Have a regular exercise routine that encompasses strength/flexibility/endurance (this is also a metaphor lived through the body) and pay more attention to the impact of your thoughts and emotions on your physiology.

3. No matter how old you are, define the elements of your ideal.

4. Identify limiting beliefs, identify the source of your beliefs, and understand the difference between beliefs and the truth.

5. Come up with two possible solutions for every problem you envision.

6. Make sure you understand *why* you have set a goal and not just examine the *how* to accomplish it.

CHAPTER FIVE
THE COURAGE TO BUILD BRIDGES

Strength is granted to us all when we are needed to serve great causes.

—*Winston Churchill*

Courage is a word with many definitions, shapes, and sizes. There are acts of bravery that fall under the idea of self-preservation. We read stories about hikers trapped on a mountain who have to cut off a limb in order to survive. Or we encounter abused women at shelters who have fled a harmful relationship with no money and only the clothes on their back. The stories fill headlines.

We've also had to learn the meaning of courage in our own lives. Our experience, we hope, exemplifies the kind of courage that aligns itself with personal growth: Nina pushing herself to confront her greatest fear and take public speaking courses. Mary Beth trading in a lifetime of sitting on the sidelines of soccer fields, in auditoriums watching ballet recitals, and in front of the TV admiring Olympic competitors to confront her own fear of swimming and aversion to running and take the plunge into the sport of triathlon. Her courage experience was athletic, but to Mary Beth it served as metaphor for finding the courage within to forge her own new journey and help carry herself and her children across the finish line during a difficult and challenging time in their lives.

These strivings for personal best are challenging and, yep, they do require us to face some personal demons or anxieties. Who can't help but marvel when we hear about an athlete who, after defeat upon defeat, finally crossed the finish line to win. Or the senior who went back to college to get the degree he never thought was possible. These people have guts.

But in this chapter we explore yet another kind of courage. That is the courage to reach out to others in a time of need and to perform selfless acts for the benefit of others. If fear is largely about feeling alone and frightened, then the kind of selfless courage where people reach out and connect to another, or to a community of others, brings a whole new emotional definition to the word *courage*.

Consider a brother who raises his siblings after his parents' death. Or a successful businessman who volunteers his time as a hospice worker helping others face their fear of death and helping them live fully to the end. These are some of the stories you will find in this chapter. They tell the story of a kind of courage that connects all humanity.

Sometimes, when we are facing our own struggles and difficulties, it pays to remember that others are trapped in their own fears too. When we reach out with courage and offer a hand across the bridge of pain and suffering, we do much for justice and human dignity.

CHANCES ARE: FOLLOWING THE DEATH OF HIS PARENTS, HE STEPS UP SPIRITUALLY AND EMOTIONALLY TO CARRY ON AND CARRY FORWARD HIS SIBLINGS

God, grant me the serenity to accept the things I cannot change, the courage to change the things I can, and the wisdom to know the difference.

—Reinhold Niebuhr

Musician, producer, music instructor, and divorced father of three daughters ages five, eight, and 10, Christopher Brickman exudes cheeriness and affability. A resident of Windsor, Wisconsin, this 38-year-old Grateful Dead fan with big soulful eyes and an even bigger smile wasn't always serene.

Growing up in Racine and Appleton, Wisconsin, Chris remembers his childhood as idyllic and joyous. He describes his parents as "one of those rare couples who just seemed to have it right, straight from the beginning—not once did either of my siblings or I ever see them fight, or argue."

Life as they knew it changed on August 20, 1993, when his parents, Marc and Susan Brickman, accompanied friends on a boat trip across Lake Michigan from Waukegan, Illinois, to Saugatuck, Michigan, to celebrate their 22nd wedding anniversary.

On the lake, idling in two-to-three-foot waves, they waited for the other boats to catch up. After waving the other boats ahead, they noticed that the engines were making strange noises. Upon investigation, they were stunned to see that the boat was rapidly taking on large amounts of water. They tried to counter it with the bilge pump, and manual bailing. Then the engine quit, and they knew it was a matter of minutes before the boat would go under. Marc Brickman fired off a flare gun in the direction of the now departed boats, and then the boat's occupants were forced into the water to avoid being sucked down with the boat.

The owners of the boat, both 33, survived after spending 24 hours in the frigid 55-degree water and were rescued by the Coast Guard. Tragically, Marc and Susan, 40 and 41 respectively, after hanging on to a makeshift raft for 15 hours, passed away before the Coast Guard rescue boat arrived. Marc and Susan Brickman died on their 22nd wedding anniversary.

They left behind three children: Chris, 21, Zach, 18, and the youngest, Casey, 14.

Chris was living in Hollywood, California, at the time,

113

working at recording studios and film studios. When he got the news, he instantly knew what he had to do, and that was to return to Racine to take care of his 14-year-old sister.

"When it comes to how I felt knowing that I should take care of my sister, I'd have to tell you honestly that I don't know," Chris Brickman remembers. "I don't feel as if that subject ever entered my mind. I simply knew that this was what I was supposed to do. In many ways, it was similar to how I dealt with my parents' death. It simply was the way things were."

"As my parents were no longer around to raise her, I believed it was my duty to provide the same continuity, with the same type of structure," he recounts. "I felt I needed to be strong for those around me, and certainly the funeral experience solidified that viewpoint. People around me, and relatives included, were just crumbling. I had to summon all of my courage to help support others around me."

He experienced many fearful moments, including struggles with the insurance companies, which claimed they couldn't pay out life insurance policies since his father, Marc's, body had never been recovered. His mother's assets were payable to her husband, and likewise couldn't be distributed because Marc's death had not been certified.

Additionally, it turned out that some of the people

involved in procuring the life insurance for the family had not behaved ethically in a shared business deal, embezzling the family out of over $200,000.

Eventually, Chris began to settle into his new existence, and then slowly his own issues in dealing with this traumatic event emerged. He remembers: "Every morning, after getting my sister off to school, I would go back to bed. And every third night, I would have the same dream. In it, one or both of my parents would be present, and I would react to their presence with complete shock and surprise, as I knew that in reality they were dead. I would bring this fact up to them, to which they would laugh and say, 'Oh, Chris, we're not dead! Look, we're right here!'— all the while smiling and laughing, and even going so far as to have me hug them so that I would know that they were in fact alive, and physically real.

"Faced with this seeming undeniable truth (in the dream), I would think to myself, Well, then, all that other stuff about them dying, *that* must've just been a dream! And then of course this huge wave of relief would rush over me, this rush of ecstasy. At that moment, inevitably, I would wake up—in my parents' bed, in my parents' house. The accompanying realization, that I was there because they were dead, was truly like being told for the first time, every time, as I had believed the dream so completely."

This test of his courage was like being kicked in the stomach every morning. One morning, after a particularly agonizing dream, Chris found himself crying, pleading with his demons to make these dreams stop. Suddenly, at that moment, he heard playing from his parents' clock radio the song "Chances Are," by Johnny Mathis.

"When I told this story to my brother and sister, they both burst into tears: my parents had always considered this particular song 'their song,' " he recounts. "There is a bar in northern Wisconsin where they would occasionally go while on snowmobile trips, named Chances Are, and of course they had that song on the jukebox, and invariably, no matter how many or how few people were in atten- dance, my father would sing that song to my mother."

Chris explains that he had never changed the station on his parents' clock radio; it was tuned to the same static-filled, Spanish-language station that his parents had left it on. Also, he hadn't set the alarm. "And I had never heard that particular song on the radio before!" Chris insists. "The song played through the radio as clear as crystal, and when it ended, it went straight back to static-filled Spanish news broadcasting!"

After another occurrence of the dream and another incident with the clock radio, Chris became convinced that his parents' spirits were communicating with him. And with that realization, the dreams stopped.

"This most certainly made it much easier to cope, much easier to get through life, feeling as if I had angels watching out for me—my own personal guardians who loved me, and were still alive, in some sense of the word," he says. "This was profoundly strengthening. I saw indicators of this phenomenon manifesting nearly every day, and frankly, I still do. This simple realization, that when we pass on, we don't really 'die,' but live on in some new form, with the ability to still interact with our loved ones in some way, was empowering. It was a game-changer, as they say."

Chris is reassured that there is a spirit, a higher power that cares for each of us on this planet. And he believes that that spirit does not give us more to deal with than we are able to handle, somehow.

He says, "Even if it's a day-by-day thing, where we don't know how we'll get beyond today, very often something shows up at the last minute, in our darkest hour, to help us through with what we need. I've been 'saved' in such a manner countless times now. So much so, in fact, that I've almost come to expect it!"

POWER PRACTICE

Open yourself up to miracles. As we age, some of us become more cynical. Others, burdened by their everyday responsibilities, become blinded to spiritual messages. The next time you experience a moment of grace, instead of chalking it up to coincidence, take the time to explore it, and open your heart and mind to the possibility that a departed loved one is sending you a message or attempting to help you from beyond the grave.

PASSAGES: WITH COMPASSION AND COURAGE, HE HELPS THE DYING SAY A PEACEFUL GOODBYE AND DISCOVERS THE KEY TO LIVING FULLY

To everything there is a season, and a time to every purpose under the heaven: A time to be born, and a time to die; a time to plant, a time to reap.

—from the Bible, Ecclesiastes 3:1, put to music by Pete Seger

The truth is that everyone will die at some point, but most people prefer not to think about it. Others have a deep, abiding fear of death, which, taken to the extreme, leads to the conclusion that life is meaningless.

A healthy way to deal with this fear is to make the most of our time here, and to prepare for our own death. In fact, today, many people are preparing for dying a "good death" by getting their spiritual lives in order before they pass away.

A courageous way to deal with this fear is to help others live gracefully when their only hope is a peaceful ending.

Roy Remer, 47, of Alameda, California, is a compas-
sionate soul who, until recently, was a longtime and
revered sales representative for a book distributor. He now
works for the Zen Hospice Project, an organization that
he volunteered for many years as a caregiver to the dying.
In addition to serving on their board of directors, training
new volunteers, and facilitating support groups, Roy
can be found on the C-2 hospice ward at Laguna Honda
Hospital in San Francisco every Tuesday evening.

"Prior to serving as a volunteer caregiver to the dying, I was fearful of death and dying," Roy Remer admits. "After my experiences with people at the end of their life, I now view death as an integral part of life. I have a relationship to death in my daily life."

Roy relates that when his grandmother Bubbe Sylvia reached the end of her life, he felt powerless to help her die when she was ready and in the way she wanted. "Bubbe was fearful of going into a nursing home," he remembers. "She knew she was ready to go, however, the focus was on keeping her alive regardless of what she wanted. At that time, I knew nothing of hospice. Later on, after she died, during my process of grieving, I met a couple of Zen Hospice volunteers who encouraged me to take the training and serve."

In the past 12 years, Roy has watched people approach their death in many different ways and concludes that the fear never goes away. "Even when someone is ready to end their suffering and die, there is still fear of the unknown," he says. "For me it is no longer about getting rid of the fear, but rather about what we can do despite the fear, how we can embrace it and move on. Certainly, as the years go by and I witness more dying, there is a lessening of fear around the mystery of death, but now I have compassion for my own fear and accept it."

The Zen Hospice Project and the groundbreaking work of its founder, Frank Ostaseski, have been widely featured in the media, including the Bill Moyers television series *On Our Own Terms,* the PBS series *With Eyes Open, The Oprah Winfrey Show*, and many others.

The innovative approach at Zen Hospice Project, which has been internationally recognized, is one of mindful support of the dying. There is a lot to be done for someone who is debilitated and at the very end of their life. We can busy ourselves with tasks: bringing water, puffing a pillow, and such. But Roy believes that in order to act as a grounded presence for someone, one must accept the inevitability of his or her own demise.

"I witness a death knowing that in the big picture, I am right behind the person who is dying before me. No one knows how soon after I will follow. We are on this journey together. This is why these people whom I sit with are such powerful teachers. They are showing me the way. Even the ones who resist, who have not made peace with their lives, are still my teachers, simply because they are departing this world before me, and there is something to learn about the process."

Roy theorizes that some people's fear of dying may stem from a lack of peace with how they have lived their life. "Perhaps they have not healed their relationships, or forgiven themselves for things they never accomplished," he says. "So for all of us, confronting the inevitability of death helps us to make peace with the life we have led."

Roy has observed that the people who spend their final days, weeks, or months in Laguna Honda's 24-bed hospice ward, the last open ward in the United States, show a tremendous amount of bravery.

"When I bring the morgue gurney onto the ward after a death, I notice some who avert their eyes and others who confront it. In any case, they all find their way of dealing with all the death around them. A couple of Tuesdays ago, four people died throughout the day and evening, all while the others are living their lives as best they can."

To Roy, courage means to experience suffering, one's own or another's, and not push it away. "As humans, we are very clever about pushing away or avoiding suffering," he says. "To develop forbearance in regard to suffering is to develop courage. I have felt most courageous during moments of extreme vulnerability and not-knowing. By taking on the great mystery of death as a teacher, I have learned that we do not always need to know or be in control, we only need to be open to whatever unfolds before us."

POWER PRACTICE

Roy Remer's advice to others facing loss is to fully experience whatever comes up. Do not push away anger, sadness, fear, or helplessness, or plan to deal with it later. Be compassionate toward yourself and whatever arises. Find an anchor in your breath and just hold on, one breath at a time.

Remember that you have everything you need to deal with the crisis; you do not need to be anything other than who you are right at this moment. Sometimes vulnerability is the most courageous attitude.

AFTER THE TSUNAMI: DEFYING CULTURAL MORES AND CREATING A NEW CULTURE TO HELP OTHERS AFTER CATASTROPHES

I am not afraid of storms, for I am learning to sail my ship.

—Louisa May Alcott

At the end of 2004, after much deliberation, Patra Rina Dewi, 32, a cellular biologist, was ready to answer her professor's call to pursue her doctoral studies at a university in Malaysia. The aspiring PhD candidate was at home in Padang, Indonesia, visiting her parents and readying documentation to chart her new course.

But Patra's life changed in an instant when she woke up on December 26th to the horrific TV reports. A cataclysmic tsunami had struck, claiming hundreds of thousands of lives and displacing an equal number of others throughout Indonesia. It was one of the most deadly disasters in modern history. When Patra heard about the people in the tiny fishing villages that were closest to the epicenter and the hardest hit, she was desperate to help. The remote islands that dot the Indian Ocean off Sumatra are, or were, a tropical paradise of white sandy beaches and clear water and home to "the perfect wave" for surfers who trekked there from across the globe.

Desperate fishermen there were getting very little help from major rescue operations. Patra could not ignore the news reports that streamed in describing overwhelming suffering and loss: a young father whose wife and newborn were swept away moments after the birth; families whose homes and possessions were destroyed, leaving them with no food, water, or livelihood; young children stricken with malaria, tuberculosis, and myriad post-tsunami ailments caused by poor sanitation; traumatic memories of hundreds of bodies floating offshore.

Call it providence or coincidence. Patra and her sister, Ulya Uti Fasrini, 26, who was studying to be a medical doctor, and a group of their friends crossed paths with a group of California surfers. The disparate team of surfers, American journalists, the sisters, and their Muslim friends joined together to make a difference. They headed out on an 85-foot diesel-powered yacht called the Mikumba. *The problem was, the religion of Islam forbids young women to travel in such close proximity to Muslim men, not to mention surfer dudes from Los Angeles and San Fran-*

cisco. Plus, Patra says, she was *"very concerned"* because she was timid and spoke very limited English.

"I was just following my heart at the time, like my sister did. We never knew each other," she says speaking about the surfers. *"We just jumped on the boat as a team."*

Today, six years later, the once timid but self-professedly stubborn Patra is a powerful trailblazer and visionary who has founded an amazing grassroots movement to help disaster victims everywhere. Forget about language barriers—these days, as the founder and executive director of Komunitas Siaga Tsunami (KOGAMI) (http://kogami.multiply.com; http://kogami.or.id), she's taking on government officials throughout Indonesia and Cambodia, demanding that education and disaster preparedness programs be put in place. The nonprofit organization started as a tsunami alert community whose mission is to educate people about disaster preparedness and how to survive disasters including earthquakes and tsunamis.

And Patra has also learned to surf, hijab *and all.*

In December 2004, with the yacht *Mikumba* set to sail the next day, Patra Rina Dewi and her sister, Ulya Uti Fasrini, told their parents about their plan to join the team of California surfers who formed the impromptu Surfzone Relief Organization (SRO). "My parents said, 'Be careful.' They have always taught us to be brave. I believe my sister never felt as scared as I did. We knew that we would be in the middle of the ocean with these strangers who we did not know before. Some friends reminded us of this, but as long as our parents felt okay, we felt okay. We truly believed their intuition."

Another challenge: their faith. "In Islam, we have some rules to protect woman from the violence including how to manage ourselves to be around the man," Patra says. Some parents teach their daughters not to be so friendly with men because they are afraid that their daughters will have sex before marriage—strictly forbidden in Islam—"or a broken heart because of man and distract the daughter's life."

"Fortunately, we have parents with high education," she adds. "My father used to work in the Education and Culture Department and my mother was a lecturer. Even though they also have rules for us, we still can have argumentation with them. We had to convince them that we could take care of ourselves."

Parental challenges tackled, the sisters set sail. The boat was one of the first rescue teams to leave Padang headed for the Mentawai Islands, and it was loaded to the gunwales with rice, dried fish, potatoes, fresh fruits, tools, medical supplies—and even live goats and dugout canoes. All these items were absolutely essential for the survival of the Sumatran island villagers.

Their voyage was spearheaded by an unlikely field commander—Matt George, at the time a 46-year-old San

Francisco journalist and contributing editor for *Surfer* magazine. George had known of these islands from previous surfing trips, and he recruited a couple of his buddies—Tony Litwak, 35, Peer Court Program Director for the California Community Disputes Services, and David Lupo, 36, an organizer for Carpenter's Union Local 22 in San Francisco—as a SWAT team to deliver supplies to these remote locales.

The surfer guys wore bandanas and shades. Patra and the women wore *hijab* (head scarves) and the modest clothing of their Muslim culture.

For two and a half weeks, the *Mikumba* team traveled from island to island, delivering 70 tons of food, water, and the other desperately needed supplies and medical services to the more than 4,000 isolated survivors. Also stacked on board were more than 60 dugout canoes, carved by Indonesians from one of the other islands. In the months to come, the team would embark on three rescue missions.

Throughout the trip, the crew had to make difficult choices. On one of the first days, after traveling about 10 hours north, they were ready to drop off the buckets of food for stranded residents. But after arriving at the first island, they found an eight-month-old boy with tuberculosis fighting for his life. The baby would die if he wasn't brought to a hospital.

"We had to make a quick decision to deliver and distribute the goods or to turn around and head back south ten hours to the hospital," George recalls. They made the choice to take the baby, his mother, and grandmother on board and head back to where they had come from. During the night, the doctors on board administered CPR four times to the child. They made it to the hospital. But despite all efforts, the little boy couldn't hold on to life.

After their journey, Patra felt compelled to ask herself, What do I do next? And she asked George and his SRO team: "What if someday Padang is hit by tsunami? Do you think Padang is ready?" They learned that Padang was a perfect target for a potential tsunami. "We started thinking that we needed to do something, but we did not know how to start. We did not have any knowledge about this hazard."

With determination and the help of George and his team, the sisters refused to let this detail stop them. KOGAMI was born. "My sister arranged a meeting with the government," Patra says. At the time, the Indonesian government did not have a disaster management system in place. "Some of them gave thumbs up, but some of them denied the possibility about another tsunami, and some of them said, 'We never have plan before disaster happens.'"

Not to be swayed by government roadblocks, the sisters vowed to stay strong and forge ahead. With the SRO's help, they taught themselves and others how to make simple evacuation plans and then went on to create larger-scale disaster preparedness programs.

In the last six years, their group has worked closely with the SRO to prepare Indonesians for catastrophe. They came to the rescue for the West Sumatra earthquake in September 2009, and in response to other disasters. Recently, Patra traveled to Cambodia to participate in a workshop on disaster risk reduction and climate change adaptation.

Today, the tagline for KOGAMI, which is also Patra's personal mantra, says it all: Let's develop a disaster-preparedness culture.

"Nobody can make exact plan in their lives including me," says Patra. "A human is not able to make exact plan for life—the tsunami hit and I just followed my heart to help. I feel that I am blessed by God that I can upgrade my knowledge and share experiences with the community especially in reducing disaster risk."

There has not been a second tsunami, but the powerful earthquake that hit in September 2009 had a magnitude of 7.6. "It was the strongest earthquake I ever felt," Patra says. "I had no worry about myself, but I was really thinking about my parents. They are old and can't move fast. Luckily, at the time, they were with me. I was driving them back home but on the way home the earthquake strike. I stopped in the middle of road until the shaking stopped. My parents agreed to go to safe area without going home to pick my sister and her daughters, three years old and nine months old, because we have agreement and evacuation plan."

She continues, "I would never forget how I could drive so calm and reach the safe area in less than thirty minutes. After I heard cancellation about tsunami warning, two hours later, I drove home and found my sister and her daughters were okay. And the next day, I went to the office to check all staff and start emergency plan. I am so happy because people were back to their normal lives three days after earthquake. This means they have resilience. They have a plan that works."

POWER PRACTICE

After facing not one but two catastrophes, Patra advises others to face life's challenges with determination and strength. Her advice is summed up on the home page of her personal website: "Shower life with love." If you are interested in practicing this, check out Finding Higher Ground, *a documentary about the amazing tsunami rescue team and the grassroots KOGAMI movement. It promises to inspire.*

COURAGE TO LOVE

To love at all is to be vulnerable. Love anything, and your heart will certainly be wrung and possibly broken. If you want to make sure of keeping it intact, you must give your heart to no one, not even to an animal. Wrap it carefully round with hobbies and little luxuries; avoid all entanglements; lock it up safe in the casket or coffin of your selfishness. But in that casket—safe, dark, motionless, airless—it will change. It will not be broken; it will become unbreakable, impenetrable, irredeemable.

—C.S. Lewis

Clive Staples Lewis (1898–1963) was an Irish-born British author, scholar of medieval literature, and Christian apologist. He is best known for his essays on Christianity and for the children's fantasy series *The Chronicles of Narnia*. His quote about the avoidance of pain beautifully illustrates how much courage it takes to love another being.

Finding the courage to love can be difficult. Call it the "L" word, or listen to those who believe the three most intimidating words in the English language are "I love you."

There is good reason to be afraid of love. Those you love can hurt you. They can betray you. They might die and you will grieve their loss. People we love can disappoint us. They can stop loving us back. They can suffer and we wish we could suffer for them. You might want to love, but don't know the right way to show it. We hurt because we wish we could love better.

Love takes courage. It is a risk. It leaves us vulnerable. And yet, nothing in life can give us as much joy as our ability to open our hearts to love.

What is true love? Why is love so frightening? Will someone ever love you as unconditionally as you want to be loved? Can you love others in a powerful way? Our daily lives present many opportunities to love. But sometimes we need the inspiration of those wiser than ourselves who have stepped up to love with humor, daring, and a belief that it is worth the risk. As Lao Tzu says: "Being deeply loved by someone gives you strength, while loving someone deeply gives you courage."

CHAPTER SIX
THE COURAGE TO FACE ADVERSITY

*Hope begins in the dark, the stubborn hope that if
you just show up and try to do the right thing, the
dawn will come. You wait and watch and work:
you don't give up.*

—Anne Lamott

We all know someone—she's the young widow next
door left to raise her small children on her own. He's the
man crossing the finish line who won his battle against
leukemia. She's the woman struggling with severe depression who still manages to lead a productive life. He's the
20-something soldier who returned from Iraq changed
forever, suffering from traumatic brain injury (TBI).

These people cross our paths and we are in awe. We
wonder how they can deal with such huge struggles and
still have the courage to forge ahead. We wonder what
qualities these people share, people who face seemingly

insurmountable physical and mental challenges yet manage to survive, and indeed to thrive.

Throughout our lives, at some time or another, we all have experiences that are challenging and seem overwhelming to us. Sometimes how we face them defines who we become. Think about it: the times when we faced our deepest fears are the moments that shaped our not only our destinies, but also our identities.

It's one of the main reasons we chose this topic for the book you are now reading. We wanted to delve into the psyches of those who have had the courage to move through tremendous adversity with hope and with the desire to learn all they can so they can help others in their journeys.

PLUMBING THE DEPTHS: TOUCHING BOTTOM SO SHE CAN HELP OTHERS STAY AFLOAT

We could never learn to be brave and patient if there were only joy in the world.

—Helen Keller

The death of a loved one is always painful. But when that person takes his or her own life, coping and healing can be even more difficult. Loved ones left behind always wonder: Could I have done more? Is it my fault? If only I had... The guilt and the what-ifs haunt them for years.

When her boyfriend took his own life, Amanda Coggin was left asking all these questions. She devoted years to understanding what she could have done differently, why he made the choice he did.

Now Amanda, a writer in San Francisco, works with friends to prevent similar tragedies, and she hopes to

undergo training in the future to lead suicide support
groups. She is writing a book about her experiences and
the gifts that came from diving into the depths of her grief.
Because she wants to encourage people to take their grief
seriously, whenever Amanda hears of someone struggling
with depression, a suicide, or death of a loved one, she
reaches out to them.

"I try to remind friends and strangers that you can't
handle something this serious on your own," she says.
"Once their loved one has died, I give the survivor left
behind my story, my number, and I tell them to call me
whenever they might find they want to. I recommend the
grief groups that helped me heal, and then I tell them to
take as much as time as they need to fully grieve, because
this culture never taught us how to make space for that
life-altering process."

Living in San Francisco and Idaho when they weren't traveling, Amanda Coggin and her boyfriend, Bryce, seemed
to have the world on a string. For four years, their lives
revolved around each other as they explored the world and
their places in it. There were signs that Bryce considered
life more of a struggle than most, but Amanda, like many
partners, was confident that her love and support would
help them navigate troubled waters.

"I remember a time in Idaho in 2006 when Bryce
described having demons in his head," Amanda recalls. "I

tried to get him to open up, but now I know that he was afraid of taking me with him. And I was too scared to go there."

Amanda went into couples therapy with Bryce after he stopped sleeping and began acting erratically. "I was terrified to talk to him about his depression and references to suicide," she says, "because I thought that if I used the word *suicide*, I would actually cause it to happen."

Amanda is not alone in this; it is a common myth that if one asks a depressed person if they are thinking of suicide, it will give him or her the idea. The fact is, if a person is suicidal he or she has already been thinking of it. If they haven't, you're not going to give them the idea.

"I grew up with a depressed mother," Amanda says, "so I finally put the pieces together and started to become aware that Bryce was depressed. In October 2006, I finally realized that this ship was sinking and I was going down with it." She decided to leave the relationship as an act of self-care.

Three weeks later, Bryce crashed a car while driving with his father. Tragically, his father was paralyzed in the accident. A few months after that, Bryce killed himself.

In the time leading up to these tragedies, Amanda joined Al-Anon, a support organization for loved ones facing addictions. There she found that she didn't really know how to take care of herself in the face of a loved one's overwhelming feelings. "At Al-Anon I found a community that wanted to help by supporting me. They used the foundation of 12-step recovery to learn that the best way to help another is to take care of yourself first. Al-Anon taught me how to reach out to others and ask for help. It also helped me understand that by fixating on my boyfriend's issues, I had lost myself."

One night in January, Amanda felt really, really anxious. "I woke up the next morning with some sort of premonition. Within an hour, I learned Bryce had taken his life."

For a decade, Amanda has practiced Vipassana meditation—the name means "to see things as they really are"—one of Asia's most ancient techniques of meditation. She credits her meditation practice with keeping her from drowning emotionally during this difficult time. She continued to meditate, joined a suicide survivors support group, attended Al-Anon meetings, became a member of the Northern California Board of Trustees of the American Foundation for Suicide Prevention, saw a suicidologist who helped her understand that she wasn't at fault, and later followed up with another grief group at San Francisco's Zen Center.

She says, "I made it my job to work through the excruciating pain. By working that hard, I was able to turn my grief into a gift."

Today Amanda is happily engaged to be married. But she may always wonder whether there is something she could have done differently, "That's the thing about suicide, no matter how much you heal, you're always left with the what-ifs." She frequently refers to the fear that paralyzed her during the relationship, and prevented her from taking action. Now that she knows herself better, and by better understanding depression and codependency, she is determined to share that knowledge with others.

Her advice for someone with a depressed partner? "Depression is the disease that nobody talks about. We need to take it from whispers and bring it to the table as conversation. Always remember, it's not your fault. Ultimately, it is another human being's choice to do with their life what they will, even if they are very sick when they make that choice. I would also encourage partners to seek outside help. There are affordable resources if you do the work your grief quietly asks you to do."

Amanda believes that "depression, like cancer, is beyond our control until we find a cure. The brain is the biggest organ in our body, but the least researched. Fortunately, with technology, that's changing."

She advises people to take threats of suicide very seriously. "Under California law, a person who is a threat to him or herself can be involuntarily confined [for 72 hours] to get help." But first, she urges, "Get help yourself by reaching out to others. You can work past fear and take action. That act of courage can help save a loved one's life. And if even after all your efforts the person decides to take their life, know that by working through your grief the benefits of processing the tragedy can help open your heart to help others."

POWER PRACTICE

Know that you are not to blame. We all carry wounds from our childhoods and from slights throughout our lives. We think it is our fault if we are the target of another person's anger or blame. It takes courage and strength to seek help to learn how to move away from the bull's-eye and learn that you are not responsible for other people's circumstances and problems. Once you take yourself out of the equation, you can see more clearly how to help the other person.

A MOTHER'S UNRELENTING COURAGE: LESSONS ABOUT RESILIENCE FROM A MOTHER DETERMINED TO FORGE AHEAD DESPITE HER FAILING MEMORY AND HEALTH

If you take a step toward life, life will support you.

—Author Phyllis Theroux, sharing the inspirational words of her aging mother in the book The Journal Keeper: A Memoir

When the mother who raised you starts slipping into a sea of forgetfulness, it can stop you in your tracks. But here, New York life coach and writer Ann Mehl shares the wisdom and newfound courage she has gained in watching the feisty way her mother is fighting back against her fading memory and the detour her life is taking because of dementia.

She says she is reminded of "the things to remember, when my mom forgets." We share Ann's story told in her own graceful way.

BY ANN MEHL

My mom hides her purse behind her pillow at night. Inside her bag is a roll of pencils, a pair of steel pliers, a wallet full of change, four hair curlers, safety gloves, a deck of playing cards, and three rubber bands. Why is her bag in that specific spot and as heavy as a box of rocks? I suspect it's because, as a child of the Great Depression, she was raised to keep your valuables close, and to throw nothing away. But if you were to ask my mom, she could not tell you why she is carrying the contents of a plumber's toolbox in her pocketbook. She probably wouldn't even recognize it as her own. My mom suffers from dementia. She's all mixed up and she knows it.

Since my father passed away over five years ago, I've watched my mother slip deeper and deeper into a shadowy fog of memory loss. The most difficult part is watching her observe the changes in herself. "I just don't know what's happening to me. I used to be so on top of things," she will often lament. Beyond historical events, her cache of recent memories is fleeting. The furniture in our home where she has lived for 36 years is unrecognizable to her. The day of the week, the month, even the year: all are beyond her powers of retention. Facts and details flit away like butterflies.

What is most remarkable—aside from the fact that modern medicine cannot find a cure—is my mom's everyday courage and resilience in the face of this cruel disease. She tries to laugh. Sometimes she is silly. And even when she doesn't know where we're headed, she willingly climbs into the car and comes along for the ride. Rarely does she get upset.

Her situation is certainly not unique. According to the Centers for Disease Control, the numbers for dementia are staggering. Worldwide, there are now an estimated 24 million people living with some form of dementia. Sooner or later, we all will deal with parents and loved ones whose health and memories are failing them. As my siblings and I learn to care for my mom, here are some of the lessons I have found to be important:

ACCEPT THEM WHERE THEY ARE.

Growing up, my mother took great pride in her family's appearance, including her own. Now I need to remind her on a daily basis to bathe or change her clothes. Although deep down you may want the younger version of your mom or dad back, try to accept your loved one and their current limitations. Concentrate on the now. I draw gratitude from the simple. I am happy that my mom is trying. She is welcoming and warm. She smiles. She is happy to spend time with her grandchildren. My mom still recognizes my voice on the phone. I no longer probe for answers, as it simply flusters her when she cannot recall the details. Instead, I am content that she trusts me to handle her personal matters. She wants to hold my hand during her doctors' visits. Mourning the loss of what she *used* to do—cooking a meal, knitting a sweater, volunteering, calling me on my birthday—only takes away from the small blessings that we still enjoy together.

PUT YOURSELF IN HER SLIPPERS.
My mom tires early in the day now and talks incessantly about when we'll next eat. She repeats herself over and over again, almost to comfort herself with the one or two tales she has not forgotten. She is fixated on making cups of tea and washing her sheets. In this flurry of manic activity, I look at her and see the woman who cleaned and cooked for five growing children; the mom who drove me from mall to mall in the hunt for the perfect prom dress. The seamstress; the diaper changer; the listener; the peacemaker. She took in a cousin and raised her as a sister. She buried a husband and cared for her own invalid mother who lived in our house for over a decade. After 75 years, I too might be confused and absent of information. I try to imagine how she feels at this stage of her life, during the moments when I begin to grow impatient with the endless questions and her pace and her wonder.

We have my mother on medication in the form of a memory patch, which she wears daily. I've contacted neurologists, who have screened my mom. Most confess to having no certain answers. We could take some more of my mom's blood, try another pill, or register her for hyperbaric oxygen chamber treatments. We will attempt some of these if time and the need warrants. For now, I'll just watch and learn from the master. She will tell me everything.

Everything she remembers, that is.

POWER PRACTICE

At times when life requires the courage to face its dilemmas, and secretly you'd rather crawl back under the covers than face and deal with these feelings, keep a journal. A journal can be a safe place to unload your fears: when you write them down, you can leave them behind on paper. It's also a place to explore your fears and try to understand them. Often a journal is where you can chronicle the insights and inspirations, the glimpses of hope that keep you going. In the words of American artist Audrey Flack: "What makes for great art is the courage to speak and write and paint what you know and care about."

A PORTRAIT OF RESILIENCE AND FORTITUDE: CREATING HOPE FOR THREE GENERATIONS OF FAMILY IN CHICAGO'S MOST DEPRESSED POCKET

The ultimate measure of a man is not where he stands in moments of comfort, but where he stands at times of challenge and controversy.

—Martin Luther King Jr.

On the gritty, gang-filled streets of Chicago's West Austin neighborhood, Lucille Jackson struggles to raise three generations of her family. She has lost three of her five children to gang violence and cancer. Now, she is raising two of her grandchildren and says, "I just pray to God to protect us."

Her prayers, like those of many others in the Austin neighborhood, one of the poorest and most crime-ridden neighborhoods of Chicago, are being answered in part by a newly opened high school. The school has given her grandson Michael hope, and provides employment for her other grandson, Victor—it is the one place where Lucille knows Michael and Victor are safe. It is part of a network of 22 schools established in inner-city neighborhoods from San Francisco to New York City.

One of the school's early supporters was Chris Gardner, self-made millionaire and author of the best seller Pursuit of Happyness, *a memoir about becoming homeless with his young son and clawing his way up, which became a hit movie starring Will Smith. During a visit to the school, Gardner conveyed a message to the students that inspires parents and grandparents like Lucille: Don't ever let someone tell you what you can't do.*

Michael, whose mother died six years ago from complications of drug use, has never known his father and was witness to his uncle's gang-related killing. These days, he not only goes to school and has plans for college; he also works at a hospital transferring patients in their wheelchairs and stretchers. "When I'm transporting them to their destination," he says, "they usually say, 'Thank God for Michael, because without him, I would be lost.' "

For Grandma Lucille, who says she feels as if she has lived under siege for decades, afraid of the gangs, drugs, and violence of her neighborhood, Michael's future is her hope. "It makes me know that what I've done has been worth it all," she says. "Michael has a future."

Lucille Jackson came to the Austin neighborhood of Chicago in 1965 with five young children in tow, bearing flower seeds: peonies, orange lilies, hibiscus, and Hostas, all ready to be planted into a garden wrapped with a white picket fence. She also had a determination to set down strong roots for her family. She was desperate to find someone to trust. For most of her life, she had lived on the edge of homelessness.

But she is no slouch. "I promised myself that my kids would never be where I had been," Jackson says.

Having dreamed since childhood of living in a house where you could hear church bells ring, she says God had the same plan when her husband, Ferris, was hired as the custodian at a Chicago Catholic parish. As part of the deal, the family would live in the three-story green house next door. That is, until the day her husband walked out, leaving Lucille to cobble together the funds to buy the house and keep a roof over her children's heads.

In the years that followed, she lost three of her five children to gang violence and cancer. These days, she raises two of her 11 grandchildren—Michael Washington, 17, and his older cousin, Victor, who is in his twenties.

"I want a future for Michael," she avers. "I tell him every day, 'You don't have to be a somebody to be anybody.' And what I mean is you don't have to have everything in the world to make something of yourself in the world."

In the summer of 2008, two events occurred to unlock the doors of opportunity for Michael. Lucille says it was "God answering my prayers again."

Watching day after day as a team of young boys tended to the tiny garden plot in front of the green house next door to the school, Fr. Christopher Devron noticed a doting woman sitting on the porch and giving the boys explicit gardening instructions. One day, he walked over to meet his new neighbors and invite them to a BBQ.

"I introduced myself and asked the woman if she knew any high-school-aged students who would like to come to our school," he recalls. "She told me she has a grandson, and pointed to Michael, but said they could never afford to send him to private school. I remember saying to her, 'Well, that's what we're here for.'"

Earlier that week, a curious Michael, en route to a nearby basketball court, had wandered past the "abandoned" school and the cleaning crew, and asked what was going on. Providence had taken hold.

If not for the school, Michael might be one of the 7,000 high school students in this area of Chicago left without a place after Austin High School closed its doors. For many of the youth in his neighborhood, especially the boys, prison is the most likely destination, Lucille says.

"I'm doing what I can, but just look," she says, pointing to a group of teens walking in the alley next to her home. "They're up to no good. I'm afraid some days to come outside the house. I am afraid they will hurt us."

These days, Michael is a smiling, fun-loving 17-year-old who knows he has the kind of opportunity that his Grandma Lucille wants for him despite the series of blows that have been dealt to his family. The same summer he learned about the new school, his uncle was shot four times in the heart on the steps of the school, right in front of Michael. And because of his slight build and short stature, Michael is frequently the target of bullies, his grandma reports.

Recently, the drum set that Michael, a budding musician, cherishes as much as the basketball that is his mainstay, was stolen out of the garage where Lucille had temporarily stored it. "Michael loves those drums, and he's good," she says. "How could they take that away from him?"

Michael says he wants to be a basketball player, but he's quick to add: "I've got a Plan B now. I'm going to be either a hospital technician or do something mechanical." Referring to his close proximity to school, he jokes, "I take small footsteps to school. But I've got big plans."

And Grandma Lucille is glowing: "As long as the school is here, we are safe. I've always told Michael, no matter what happens to you, if you lead a good life, if you give to others and don't ask for anything back, you are doing something for yourself. God is good and God will be there for you."

POWER PRACTICE

Parenting or grandparenting can be one of the most frightening roles we assume in our lives. It requires facing some of our greatest fears and, as Lucille Jackson shows us, forging ahead, no matter what. If you are a parent or grandparent, aunt or uncle, or a role model for young people, think about the areas in your life where you need to move ahead no matter how afraid you are. Think about what can happen if you do, and what might not happen if you don't. Take inspiration from Lucille and keep on keeping on, no matter what.

YOU CAN DO IT

Whatever happens, remember, you can—and will—get through it.

Do you know that mantra "Whatever doesn't kill me makes me stronger"? It's dramatic, but very true.

When you feel as if there's simply no way you can continue, that you've reached the end of your rope, just repeat to yourself: I can manage this, one step at a time.

Experts agree that what we're most terrified of is that we won't be able to manage at all, that something terrible will happen and we'll lose control. But even at that point, you have a choice. You can give up, or you can tell yourself that you are strong enough, and worthy enough, to rise up and meet this challenge, one step at a time.

Take some inspiration from the many stories of people who overcame tremendous physical challenges to achieve their dreams, like the children with disabilities who were never told that they couldn't accomplish anything they wanted. There is a universe of inspiration out there. Start with the simple belief that you will survive this day, and that you have the courage to open your mind to the possibility of a better tomorrow.

THE GOODBYE GIRL: A DAUGHTER STANDS ON THE SIDELINES AS HER ELDERLY MOM FACES THE ALMOST DAILY LOSS OF FRIENDS

To know how to grow old is the master work of wisdom, and one of the most difficult chapters in the great art of living.

—Henri-Frédéric Amiel

A way of looking at courage is to understand that it is not always the huge leaps we take in life. Sometimes, bravery is most needed in the cadence of daily living.

In our day-to-day lives, the virtue of courage is often overlooked. Courage is an attribute reserved for heroes, those larger–than-life people. But sometimes it is important to remember that most of us call on our inner strength many times in any given day.

As Helen Keller noted: "Security is mostly a superstition. It does not exist in nature, nor do the children of men as a whole experience it. Avoiding danger is no safer in the long run than outright exposure. Life is either a daring adventure, or nothing. To keep our faces toward change and behave like free spirits in the presence of fate is strength undefeatable."

Lately, Mary Beth been keeping an eye out for those who exemplify boldness and bravery in their daily living. Here is a brief glimpse at a daily reminder of courage she has been finding in the most unlikely of places—coat pockets.

BY MARY BETH SAMMONS

One of the experiences that go hand in hand with living in the ever-changing and always surprising weather extremes of the Windy City is that life becomes a revolving coat swap. Trench or Toggle? Polar fleece or Puffer?

Switching coats to meet the temperature swings is a basic need. It has also given me an insight to a larger story—the awe I have come to feel for those facing the frailties of old age. The appreciation for the courage it must take to live in daily consciousness that as you get old, the community around you changes as sharply and unexpectedly as the weather in Chicago.

For the seniors I have come to know in helping care for my elderly mother, I realize that so many of their days are punctuated with the news that yet another friend or neighbor has slipped into the afterlife. Almost daily, they must wrap themselves in a new coat—grief, loss, excitement for the opportunity to connect, anxiety about a hospitalization, joy for giggles at the Bingo table.

It came to me recently when I was driving my mom to the funeral of Guy, her friend Pat's husband and the other half of the couple who introduced my parents to each other and hung with them decades ago in their twenties: Lately, whenever I reach into one of my coat pockets, I pull out a chilling reminder of someone I have loved so much, a two-inch prayer card from the latest funeral service. These pocket-sized tributes encapsulate in a spiritual way the life of a friend, family member, or neighbor who has been a blessing in our lives.

Grief-stricken, I remember thinking my father was so small, a quiet, humble presence of a man, a tender soul whose life was largely simple and unattended—yet was so honored at his death. I wrote his tribute, editing the entirety of his being into a short summary: a man who found the blessings in every day.

My growing collection of prayer cards insinuate themselves into my pockets, my dreams, and my heart. They shake me. They scare me. They make me sad. The most obvious reason, I suppose, is that they are jarring reminders that there is no way to stop life's seasons, the birth of spring and hopeful beginnings and the dimming of the light. There is no way to stop this passing away, except to seize the opportunity to live fully in the in between. The cards remind me to do that.

But what astonishes me most is my mother and her friend's willingness to look certain death squarely in the eye, to balance the excitement of daily encounters—lunch at Eleanor's, a trip to the mall with Tilly, tickets to a play—with the anxiety that they may likely be in their last inning. And to have the courage to accept that.

Today, my mom announced that she has joined an Alzheimer's research group with a major Chicago hospital. She informed me of this because I am supposed to make sure that her brain is removed immediately following her death.

"Remember to tell them that, Mary," she said.

"I won't forget, Mom," I assured her. At the same time, I wanted to burrow myself away and cry. She's already planning for courage and giving in to her death.

I cannot exactly define my feelings except to say that they bounce between a loving pity for my mother and her dwindling circle of friends, and a constant marveling at the loyalty and attentiveness they give to each other.

There is a dichotomy here, and it is one that is implicit in every action I take concerning caring for my mother. I can control some of the controllables—the number of visits I make, the outings I plan, the in-between phone calls—and there is great satisfaction in the process and in the result. But what I can't control is that, for a senior living in a center for the elderly, daily life is punctuated with the blaring sirens of the emergency medical teams and the sight of paramedics flashing past my mom's window to aide an ailing neighbor. "They're here pretty much every day," my mom tells me.

Recently, when I accompanied my mother to Mass at her senior center, I was delighted by the sea of new friends who greeted her afterward in the church vestibule, just as I'm delighted by the community of others who beckon daily as she makes her way to the community center lunch, the laundry room, and the mailbox.

But then the moment took a twist. As we were winding our way back to her apartment, a neighbor approached the group to announce that the woman who lives just three doors down from my mom had died early that morning. She had been sick for a long time, and the paramedics had arrived late Saturday afternoon to take her to the hospital.

I watched as my mom put her hands to her heart, sucked in her breath, and tried to fight back tears. "Oh no, no..." she said. And soon a crowd of seniors had gathered on the walkway, sharing their guesses as to what had happened.

I realize I can't control this part of my mom's life. Sadness and loss are daily companions. It is what living in your eighties is like. I realize I will be miserable if I don't make peace with that. So, this week, our "outing" on my next visit will be to accompany my mom to the wake—another goodbye.

Most days, I am acutely aware of the cards that have

made a home in my coat pockets. Sometimes I feel the loneliness my mother must feel for her friends' absences, and for my father's. But they also remind me to be grateful for the role models I am finding in my mother and her friends. When I was in my twenties, I remember thinking that it took so much courage to find my way in the promise of a whole world that was out there waiting for me.

Now, when I touch the cards in my pocket, I am grateful for the astonishing lessons in the courage to face life—and the end of life—from the strong group of seniors who emanate bravery all around me.

POWER PRACTICE

What keeps you from being fully alive? Observing the dignity of dying that I have come to witness so often lately, I have contemplated the following quote and asked myself what it means to me. I hope you will too.

> *What keeps you from being fully alive is what you are most afraid to go through.*
>
> —Lawrence McCafferty

CHAPTER SEVEN
THE COURAGE TO BEGIN AGAIN

If one dream should fall and break into a thousand pieces, never be afraid to pick one of those pieces up and begin again.

—Flavia Weedn

We live in a time when millions of Americans are starting over. Many of us are reinventing ourselves at midlife after being laid off and are retraining to gain new skills for a new job. Some of us are divorced men and women for whom the prospect of reentering the dating game and seeking love again is a daunting one. Others are launching new careers, with job opportunities calling them to move across the country to places where they know no one. Widows, empty nesters, or survivors of a significant illness or cancer: life for many is changing. We are afraid, and certainly that is understandable.

Transitions are tough. Let's face it, who *really* likes or

embraces change? When we are faced with starting over or reinventing our lives, often we are afraid of experiencing another failure, or of not being able to get past our feelings of inadequacy. We hang on to what was, often afraid to see what can be.

In this chapter we take a look at the wisdom and personal experience of those who have overcome their inner and outer obstacles and challenged their fears to find healthy, happy new lives. They show us how to find the courage to look at our mistakes, accept the consequences of our choices, and forgive ourselves and move on to begin our lives anew. Whether it is reinventing a career at midlife or arriving in a new country as a high school student struggling to assimilate into all things American, these inspiring people offer tips and strategies for being brave enough to get rid of old patterns and make room for new ideas and dreams.

In the stories that follow, we address some of the rites of passage that many of us have faced—marriage, divorce, job loss, illness, and death—and look at ways we can find the courage to start over and stake a claim for our new future. The people in this chapter show us how to find clarity, conviction, and the courage to meet these obstacles and opportunities.

Imagine what it would be like if you had the courage to change the course of your life. Imagine what the future could hold. The key to all of that is courage. Through these stories, we hand you that key, the key to courage.

MAKING MISTAKES

Making mistakes is how we learn contrast, how we discern what we want and don't want in our life. As they say, pick yourself up, dust yourself off, and move on. Everyone makes mistakes, has challenges, bumps in the road. Looking back with regret blocks our movement forward to bigger and better things. Your future is up to you. Create it in each moment. Walk forward courageous in your choices.

—Debra Oakland, of Livingincourageonline.com

A REAL-LIFE JULIE AND JULIA: FORMER PUBLISHING EXEC PURSUES LIFELONG PASSION TO COOK UP A NEW DIRECTION AT 60

Don't be afraid your life will end; be afraid it will never begin.

—Grace Hannon

It had been more than 35 years since Peg Farrell graduated from college to head to the Big Apple to carve out a career in the publishing industry. The Queens, New York, native and Fordham University graduate with a bachelor of arts degree discovered quickly that dreams take slight detours.

Her first gig: assistant to an employment agency counselor who placed executive secretaries. An eternal optimist, Peg remembers looking at the bright side. "Well, at least I got some insights as to what industries were open to promoting women. Banking and insurance were out, but advertising was an industry where women could be more than a secretary!"

Next stop: a major advertising agency, in the media department, where she bought TV time for major consumer products including Pepsi, Pillsbury, Scott Paper, and Burger King. She was on her way.

In the next three decades, Peg married, had two children, and blazed a trail in the publishing industry. She spent 15 years at Time Inc., first as salesperson at Time *magazine, and then in sales management at* Life *and* Sports Illustrated. *Over the years, she became the associate publisher of* Reader's Digest, *the associate publisher of* Cosmopolitan, *the publisher who launched* Marie Claire, *publisher of* Country Living, *and finally publisher of* Family Circle.

Then, in her late fifties, fate interceded. When Family Circle *was sold Peg found herself out of a job. Let's just say that what she did next surprised more than a few people, including her husband and grown children. But mostly, herself.*

Fast approaching 60, Peg Farrell kept thinking about what she wanted to do. "Some people might be happy retiring and playing golf, or having lunch with friends, but I knew that was not for me," she says. "And I also knew that I did not want to do what I had been doing." She decided she would follow the advice she had so often given to others:

"Pursue your passion!" Since her twenties she always loved to cook, and had taken one-day cooking classes over the years, but she craved more.

If she was to pursue this dream she would have to enroll in a serious cooking education program, quite unlike the cooking classes she had taken. After looking at culinary schools, she found one that combined her love of cooking with another passion, her interest in Italian food, culture, and language. She was intrigued with the Italian Culinary Academy at the French Culinary Institute in New York City.

It was then that the "fear happened." As she recalls, "Could I take such a course of study at my age? Could I keep up physically with a program designed for people just starting out in a career? Could I learn the Italian language at my age? Could I emotionally handle what I knew I would feel being around mostly twenty-year-olds? I had grown up thinking sixty was old—and I was afraid it might be true."

But she plunged ahead and decided to take the risk. "I kept saying, I think I can, as I so often told my kids to say." She enrolled at the school and spent two months studying in New York and two months of intensive study at ALMA in Italy, followed by a "working internship" at a Michelin star restaurant in Lombardia. She studied culinary skills, as well as Italian history and language. She was also exposed to the study of Italian wine.

There were challenges: leaving behind her family and the comforts of home. She lived in tiny apartments above the kitchens in Italy, and when she was attending classes in New York, she commuted from her suburban home at dawn. The biggest challenge, however, was the language. "While we studied in New York and I had two tutors, I thought I would be able to handle it." Though the Italian instructor at ALMA spoke English fluently, often the guest chefs visiting from the 20 regions of Italy did not. Some spoke no English at all. And at Cantuccio restaurant, where she worked, the staff knew little English.

And there were other challenges. When Peg slipped on some spilled water in the kitchen in Italy, she was taken to a hospital where non-English-speaking doctors prescribed painkillers that she would need to administer to herself with a hypodermic needle. Not her thing. Unable to fully translate into Italian her lack of expertise in self-injection, she improvised by asking one of the kitchen workers back at the restaurant to give her a daily shot in the rear.

Then there was the time she accidently left her laptop on a bench while waiting for her cab, temporarily losing her sole mode of communication. The cabdriver tracked it down and a Good Samaritan returned it to her.

She says she tried to capture the spirit of youth intentionally during her six months of reinvention. "I tried to live the life of a student, staying where students would stay and trying to be spontaneous and adventurous. I loved it.

I impressed myself. I was doing this and doing it well! Just as well as the younger students."

After months of training, and ready to graduate, Peg's luck abandoned her when she was assigned to make fish stew for her final exam. "It's the one dish that I can't stand, I mean to the point that it makes me feel sick. I gag," she confesses.

These days, Peg is back home in Connecticut, a graduate of the French Culinary Institute's Italian Culinary Experience and the recipient of a diploma from the institute. Her skills have not gone to waste on friends and family. In fact, she spent the last few months of a close friend's life whipping up healthy gourmet meals during the time her friend was undergoing chemotherapy. It made Peg feel as if she was doing something meaningful for her friend.

Now, though she has been cooking up gourmet cuisine for friends and family, she is uncertain where her future lies. She just knows she had the courage to pursue a new course. "I feel proud that I pursued something I really loved and that it was an adventure," she says. "I thought that being sixty would make it difficult to do, but that wasn't the case at all. The message is one we all know: pursue your passions at any age, and don't let anything stop you, especially not age."

POWER PRACTICE

What have you always wanted to do but were afraid to try, either because you were too busy working or raising kids or it just didn't seem the sensible thing to do? Peg Farrell always loved to cook and entertain, but for 30-plus years she lived in the fast-paced world of the Manhattan publishing industry. Commuting to the city left her little time for culinary adventure.

How about you? Is there a hobby or a passion you've always longed to pursue? Are you afraid you've already put so much energy into one career that you don't have any left to pursue something new? Are you letting your age get in the way? Be inspired by Peg. You don't have to leave the country or enroll in a six-month program. Consider checking online or in your local newspaper to find a workshop or class you can take to improve your skills and test your talent. Ask yourself: What am I waiting for? Why am I afraid to try this? The answers may surprise you.

IMMIGRANT STUDENT FACES THE UNKNOWN AND FORGES A NEW FUTURE

One isn't necessarily born with courage, but one is born with potential. Without courage, we cannot practice any other virtue with consistency. We can't be kind, true, merciful, generous, or honest.

—Maya Angelou

Like many immigrant students new to America, Katie (her American name) Do knew little English when she arrived in San Francisco from Vietnam. A high school freshman at the time, she faced isolation due to the language barrier and the simple challenges of assimilating into American teen culture. Katie feels fortunate to be in America, but it has been a hard, scary journey.

"There were moments that I felt like giving up because of the obstacles." Katie says. "In facing the unknown, my advice is to remain calm and patient, because when you overreact to a situation you won't be able to make a wise decision." Here, she shares her story.

Katie Do's first 13 years growing up in Vietnam were full of hardship, but when the family was given the opportunity to move to the United States, she was understandably apprehensive.

A year before Katie's birth, her father was released from jail, having been sentenced by the Vietnamese communists for working alongside the US-supported South Vietnamese. While he was incarcerated, his family faced rampant discrimination and lacked provisions for everyday survival.

Katie grew up without the amenities most American children take for granted: toys, new clothes, snacks, and television. But, she says, "I was a happy child who enjoyed playing on the white sand of a nearby river, picking wild fruits up on the hill, eating sugarcane, and playing hide-and-seek with other kids in the neighborhood."

As Katie grew older, she was aware of how hard her parents had to work in the rice and sugarcane fields all day and into the night to support the family. "Unfavorable weather sometimes destroyed most of the rice and sugarcane," she recounts. "My older sisters got married and moved away, so every day after school I cleaned the house, cooked the rice, and fed the animals on our small farm."

All that changed in 1995, when Katie's family was approved to emigrate to the US. Katie did not want to leave her older sisters who stayed behind with their families. She was terrified—facing a completely unknown future in a foreign country with very limited language skills. When her family arrived in San Francisco, so many things were new to her, including riding in automobiles.

According to Katie, her greatest challenge as a high school freshman was her English-speaking ability. "I remember one embarrassing moment in art class," she recalls. "I was sitting at the same table with a couple of other girls for a project. Another student dropped her money on the floor and asked me if I took it. I replied, 'I don't see it.' But she thought I said 'I don't say' and got upset and claimed that I took it. She was very loud, so other people in the classroom turned to look at us. Eventually someone spotted the money on the floor. It was over, but I never forgot that embarrassing moment and how scared it made me feel."

Katie overcame the challenges she faced and went on to graduate from high school with honors. Now a college graduate, she works in the finance department at Clorox in Oakland, California.

Her advice to others who find themselves transplanted into a foreign culture for the first time is to work hard and don't give up. "Whether language, money, or relationships, if you think positively and work hard, most likely you'll overcome everything. Also, there were moments when I felt overwhelmed, but I tried to remind myself to be grateful for all of my blessings—then I was able to get back on track."

Create a safe place in your imagination. When you find yourself in a state of confusion, stop for a minute and imagine yourself in a calm, peaceful, familiar place. Or think about being wrapped in the arms of someone who has only your best interests at heart.

A CHECKLIST TO JUMP-START YOUR REINVENTION

For months, Michele Woodward kept hearing the same question from many of her female clients who came to her office frazzled and frightened: "What's next?" The Washington, DC, master-certified life coach decided to pull together a group of women in midlife to meet three times a month and explore that existential angst: "Am I really happy? What is next for me?"

They came from all walks of life—a CEO of a real estate investment group, a mom of teens leaving home for college, an executive director of a nonprofit, and others. At first they came to commiserate, then to support each other and get clear about who they were and what they wanted to do. Next, they created a workable plan to do it.

The common bond: "They all were terrified about what's next," Woodward says. Mentoring each other, they met week after week throughout the spring and summer to create a plan to reinvent themselves. For some, it was changing careers, for others, finding more fulfillment in their current role, or improving the work–life balance.

Out of their experience, Woodward offers this checklist of tips for answering the "What's next?" question and jump-starting your reinvention:

1. Ask yourself: What do you want more than anything right now? You have an immediate answer, don't you? That's your gut talking to you. And you immediately reject your gut feeling, because it is sometimes frightening, or it's hugely inconvenient, or it's not what you're supposed to want.

2. Trust your gut. If you want to feel better—more passionate, happier, alive—you have to pay attention to that poor little rejected feeling. Because the first glimmer is the key to unlocking whatever it is that's holding you back.

3. Get clear about what you want. Envision it. Believe you've actually achieved it.

4. Take stock of your strengths and make a list of what you are good at. The CEO, for example, discovered that her strength was working in turnaround companies, reorganizing them and driving their success. Realizing this, she knew what to look for in her next job, Woodward says.

5. To change or reinvent yourself, you have to get over the "What will people think?" issue. Do what makes *you* happy.

6. Accept that change is scary.

7. Find mentors. Despite their different backgrounds and paths of reinvention, the women in this group became mentors and encouragers for each other.

8. Take action.

9. Engage in self-care. During the process of reinvention, it is important to care for yourself and to be compassionate with yourself during the transformation.

10. Stay connected with your supporters both through and after the reinvention.

Michele Woodward shares her coaching insights on her website: www. lifeframeworks.com.

HOW ONE MAN'S COURAGE CHANGED HIS COURSE AND IS CHANGING THE WORLD, ONE STUDENT AT A TIME

One must always be prepared for riotous and endless waves of transformation.

—Louise Glick

In May 2010, Jim Ziolkowski was in the South Bronx participating in a service rally with more than 150 high school students. The students had fanned out across the community to clean up abandoned parking lots, distribute food and clothing to the elderly and the homeless, and host a craft fair for low-income children. One team was feeding a group of more than 100 people in a church basement. All of those who were fed and given a full bag of groceries were HIV-positive or had AIDS.

"I could just feel the compassion of the students," Jim says. The South Bronx neighborhood of New York

is described as the poorest congressional district in the United States. "The people we served are not only battling HIV and AIDS, they are battling poverty. Our students let each of them know that they are not alone and that we care. They lifted up the people through their smiles, their kind words, and their actions."

Jim envisaged this dream more than 20 years ago when he founded buildOn.org, an international organization that empowers high school students to change lives worldwide. Student by student, the urban youth have touched the lives of over 1.4 million elderly, homeless, disabled, and young people in need. His experience with the students in the South Bronx speaks volumes about how buildOn.org has sparked an educational revolution in urban America and across the world, from the East Coast to Nepal, Brazil, Nicaragua, and beyond.

As President and CEO of buildOn.org, Jim has led the organization in building 340 schools in developing countries and launching almost 120 after-school enrichment programs in schools across the US. He does this by rallying high school students facing their own tremendous adversity to reach out and help others who are also struggling. The result is hope and optimism in places where there is little.

Most significantly, Jim's story is the story of one man who found the courage to follow his daring vision. It leaves all of us with a bold challenge: If we can find the

courage, we can attempt to change what seems unchange-
able. Here is how the career of one man who had the guts
to leave his corporate career to create a bright and better
future for others unfolded.

In 1990, Jim Ziolkowski spent a year backpacking across
the globe. Six days up on a trek in the mountains of Nepal,
he stumbled on a community celebrating the opening of a
new school they had built with their own hands. "They
celebrated for two days, forty-eight straight hours, that's
how excited they were," Jim remembers. He came home
from the 12-month sabbatical and realized that he needed
to get back to real life and work. So he donned pinstripes
and took a high-powered job in the finance department
of GE.

But the celebration he observed in the mountains
tugged at him. He couldn't stop dreaming about the
outpouring of pride he witnessed from the villagers. It
challenged his thoughts daily and soon would change the
course of his life. He started to develop a vision: What
about helping teens help teens? What about empowering
urban youth from difficult circumstances not only to make
a positive difference in their own communities, but to
help enhance education and opportunities for their peers
in impoverished nations across the globe? The idea was
simple: teens would gain self-reliance through education.
The organization would work to impart three core

values: compassion, responsibility, and empowerment.

The Michigan State University graduate took the leap and quit his nine-to-five job at GE, launching buildOn.org.

Working closely with his brother David, Jim set off to Brazil, Malawi, and Nepal to build the first three schools. Once they were built, Jim continued working alongside villagers for several more years to develop a methodology that would empower the world's poorest communities to build their own schools. At the same time, he created unique after-school programs and an interconnecting methodology that engages US students in serving their own communities and empowers them to help build schools worldwide.

During the almost 20 years since he left corporate America to forge his nonprofit, Jim has been strongly influenced by personal meetings with Mother Theresa and the Dalai Lama. But he says he has been most profoundly influenced by the youth he has worked with, from America's biggest cities to the poorest villages on the planet. He says it is the students' courage and thirst for education that inspire him every day.

Jim does not feel he has had courage; instead he says he is inspired all the time by the people he encounters across the world. Here he describes a recent moving experience in connection with traveling to Nicaragua with a group of high school students from Detroit:

"I was en route to Nicaragua and the tiny mountain

village of La Soledad—way up near the border of Honduras. The community was founded fifty years ago by a small group of families seeking refuge from war. There are now more than 450 people living in this jungle village, and one hundred dedicated children pack into a tiny shack every day to attend classes. The children of La Soledad have faithfully gone to 'school' for twenty years while, year after year, their parents patched, repaired, or rebuilt their shaky school. We are headed to La Soledad to work with all of the families and build their first permanent school. A school that will last for at least one hundred years.

"I stopped in Detroit to meet up with a team of buildOn students who have committed to the same journey and purpose. They are leading a movement of youth in Detroit who face and overcome daunting challenges every day to lift up the city through service. Though they concentrate on Detroit, their dedication to service and education is not confined by city limits or even national boundaries. These youth also want to change the world.

"Yesterday I was told one of the students would need help getting to the airport and might be a little late. Her mother was recently carjacked at gunpoint.

"I've been involved in buildOn for nineteen years now and I have come to believe that *all* people, regardless of circumstance, can work together to make positive and lasting change. I am always humbled by the courage, resilience, and dedication of the buildOn community. And I am always inspired by their ability to rise up and meet the challenges of making change. Being carjacked at gunpoint might slow them down but it will not stop them!"

POWER PRACTICE

In demonstrating how one man's vision and ability to reinvent himself and his career can change so many lives, Jim's story asks all of us to look for one thing in our lives that seems unchangeable but needs to be changed. And to have the guts to take action to change it. Maybe it is volunteering to read books to students at an after-school program. Or looking in the local newspaper for a community service project. It takes courage to reach out and make a difference. But we all can do it. We just need to take the first step.

CHAPTER EIGHT
THE COURAGE TO FIGHT

With courage you will dare to take risks, have the strength to be compassionate, and the wisdom to be humble. Courage is the foundation of integrity.
—Keshavan Nair

Why do some people seem to have the courage to face trials and come out the other side standing strong? Think about the people you know who have been faced with a life-threatening event or illness and who have confronted their situations with strength and grace.

These days, many of us find ourselves in situations where we need a little inspiration on the resiliency front. Some of us are facing fallout from the economy, a lost job or a foreclosed house. Others, a lousy diagnosis or chronic illness, a fractured relationship, addictions, violence, and other uncertainties. When these most terrible of circumstances happen, it can feel like the world is closing in on us.

So how do we muster the courage to face life's challenges with courage and determination? Experts who have studied the phenomenon of survival say that survivors, and "thrivers," as we call them, have certain traits in their personality that help them overcome difficult situations from everyday stresses to major life challenges. Those who have lived through these challenges also agree that the capacity for courage has been paramount in finding renewed hope, much-needed energy, and the ability to lift their spirits once again.

The good news is that courage is a survival skill that can be learned. And if we learn how to tap into our inner courage, it can lead to increased success at work, improved relationships, and a vastly brighter outlook on the future. As Joseph Campbell writes in *The Power of Myth:* "The courage to face the trials and to bring a whole new body of possibilities into the field of interpreted experience for other people to experience—that is the hero's deed."

We've learned that even when the worst happens, the human spirit can survive and thrive. Moreover, trying circumstances show what we are made of. As the American patriot Thomas Paine said when it looked as though the American colonists were going to lose the War of Independence, "These are the times that try men's souls: The summer soldier and the sunshine patriot will, in this crisis, shrink from the service of his country; but he that stands by it now, deserves the love and thanks of man and woman."

At that time, some were giving up and walking away because the struggle was getting tough. Thomas Paine was really saying, "This is how we'll see what your spirit is really made of."

In this chapter, we focus on people who have been courageous in the face of extreme adversity and tragedy. We are inspired by the will and fortitude of these ordinary people who survived extraordinary experiences.

I AM SICK AND TIRED
OF BEING SICK AND TIRED.

—Fannie Lou Hamer

Young people today are lectured that they owe their freedoms to those people who risked their lives so that the rest of us could have the benefit of basic human rights. It is hard to find a more dramatic example of this than Fannie Lou Hamer, a former Mississippi sharecropper who changed the face of democracy.

Fannie Lou Hamer was born on October 6, 1917, the youngest child of sharecroppers in Montgomery County, Mississippi. Although she was short and walked with a limp after contracting polio as a child, her mother always told her to "stand up no matter what the odds." At age six, Fannie Lou began helping her parents in the cotton fields. By the time she was 12, she was forced to drop out of school and work full time to help support her family.

Hamer became involved in the civil rights movement when she volunteered to attempt to register to vote in 1962. By then 44 years old and a mother, she was unaware that African Americans actually had a constitutional right to vote. When the SNCC (Student Nonviolent Coordinating

Committee) asked for volunteers to go to the courthouse to register to vote, Hamer was the first to raise her hand. She later reflected, "The only thing they could do to me was to kill me, and it seemed like they'd been trying to do that a little bit at a time ever since I could remember."

On June 3, 1963, Fannie Lou Hamer and other civil rights workers arrived in Winona, Mississippi, by bus. They were ordered off the bus and taken to Montgomery County Jail. Hamer recalls, "Then three white men came into my room. One was a state highway policeman (he had the marking on his sleeve). They said they were going to make me wish I was dead. They made me lay down on my face and they ordered two Negro prisoners to beat me with a blackjack. That was unbearable. The first prisoner beat me until he was exhausted, then the second Negro began to beat me. I had polio when I was about six years old. I was limp. I was holding my hands behind me to protect my weak side. I began to work my feet. My dress pulled up and I tried to smooth it down. One of the policemen walked over and raised my dress as high as he could. They beat me until my body was hard, till I couldn't bend my fingers or get up when they told me to. That's how I got this blood clot in my eye—the sight's nearly gone now. My kidney was injured from the blows they gave me on the back."

Despite this, Hamer spoke frequently to raise money for the movement, and helped organize the Mississippi Freedom Democratic Party. In 1964, the MFDP challenged the all-white Mississippi delegation to the Democratic Convention, and in 1968 the convention seated an integrated challenge delegation from Mississippi. Working with the National Council of Negro Women and others, Hamer helped organize food cooperatives and other services and also helped to convene the National Women's Political Caucus in the 1970s.

Fannie Lou Hamer died on March 15, 1977. One of the civil rights leaders who spoke at the funeral was Andrew Young, former US ambassador to the United Nations and mayor of Atlanta, Georgia. He said, "Women were the spine of our movement. It was women going door-to-door, speaking with their neighbors, meeting in voter-registration classes together, organizing through their churches, that gave the vital momentum and energy to the movement. Mrs. Hamer was special but she was also representative. She shook the foundations of this nation."

THE WILL TO SURVIVE: LESSONS IN COURAGE FROM A TEENAGER'S EXPERIENCES IN NAZI DEATH CAMPS

There may be times when we are powerless to prevent injustice, but there must never be a time when we fail to protest.

—Elie Wiesel

Courage. Stripped down to its starkest, barest essence. When there is, literally, nothing left but the courage to survive.

The Holocaust, one of the darkest chapters in history, directly affected many post-WWII immigrants and their families. But from the perspective of the authors' comfortable, late-20th-century childhoods, it seemed so distant, so unfathomable.

How did these survivors find the inner strength to endure relentless brutality without giving up? How could anyone experience the remorseless cruelty and terror of the Nazis' genocidal atrocities and then go on to live a "normal" life?

William B. Helmreich, author of Against All Odds, *found that many Holocaust survivors went on to live productive lives despite their trauma. He theorized that some of the traits that helped them survive, such as flexibility and courage, may have contributed to their later success.*

He wrote that the Holocaust survivors were no different from the rest of us. "They were ordinary individuals before the war, chosen by sheer accident of history to bear witness to one of its most awful periods."

Eli Rosmarin was an ordinary 16-year-old in September 1939, when the Germans invaded his town of Sosnowiec, Poland. Now 87, he resides in Pompano Beach, Florida, with his wife of 55 years. His story is a remarkable example of the ability of the human spirit to transcend atrocities through daily acts of courage and faith in the future.

"I was born in a very small, impoverished town called Wolbrom, in Poland," Eli recounts. "My parents had seven children who survived infancy: my oldest sister, Pesla, then Henry, Abram, Fela, Leo, me, and the youngest, Zlata. In 1935, we moved to a city called Sosnowiec, which had a population of more than a hundred thousand. Between the ages of twelve and sixteen, I worked odd jobs while I attended school."

That all changed once the Germans invaded in 1939. Eli recounts that the Nazis initially approached the local Jewish organization and asked for a few hundred men to serve as laborers during the war effort, disguising the fact that the war effort included plans to extinguish all Jews. The organization asked Jewish families for volunteers.

"Abram and Leo both volunteered to go first but Abram was the one who went," Eli remembers. "Over the course of the year, the Nazis returned, seeking additional young Jewish men. Leo went next. Both Abram and Leo were detained in concentration camps by 1940. By 1942, the few remaining Jews in the city were forced to move to the ghetto. Those in the ghettos were turned into forced laborers. While coming home from work one day, Henry was snatched off the street and sent to a concentration camp. A year later, when they came for more Jews, my father gave them Fela and me.

"While I was gone, the Nazis took the remaining ghetto residents to the gas chambers in Auschwitz, and I never saw my parents or my oldest and youngest sisters again."

Eli was first sent to a work camp called Graditz. "We were working on the rivers—damming the river or making the banks better graded. In a work camp, you can wear your own clothes, the food was better," Eli recalls. "Later, when we got to the concentration camp, we had to wear prisoner's clothes, and our rations were reduced to a piece of bread and a little soup in the evening. They also cut our hair and shaved a thin strip down the center of our heads so we would be easily recognizable if we tried to escape."

He learned a number of survival strategies while in the camp. "I didn't eat the bread in the evening; I saved it until the next morning. I could not work in the fields if I was weak with hunger so I learned to save the bread until I needed it."

"When we came to the concentration camp Fünfteichen, we were all four brothers together again. It was like a miracle. If any of us had more food from better jobs, we shared what we had. Then came news that the Russians were getting closer. The Germans moved the prisoners toward Munich to ensure that the Russians could not liberate us."

Eli describes a living nightmare of a forced marches and merciless shootings. "It was February and very cold. The Nazis forced us to march for four days. When night came, we stayed in barns they found that were so small there wasn't enough room for anyone to sit. We had to stand all night. It was unimaginable. People were fainting because there wasn't enough air to breathe. Some could not handle the frigid march and sat or lay down to rest. Then right away you would hear the gunshots."

He continues, "Under those conditions, many prisoners' minds shut down. I kept telling myself to stay alive and keep going. It never came to my mind to sit or lie down. It would have been suicide."

They stopped at a camp called Gross-Rosen, a concentration camp near the German town of Striegau in Lower Silesia (now Strzegom, Poland) that sent many prisoners to a killing center. This camp was like a hub. From there, the Nazis distributed prisoners to other camps. "We were there for about two weeks," Eli remembers.

"At the next camp, the Nazis announced they needed carpenters or machine operators. Because we were four brothers, Abram suggested that we split into two groups of two. Abram thought that there would be a better chance of at least two of us surviving by going to different camps. So Abram and I answered the call for mechanics."

Henry and Leo were sent to Flossenbürg, but they would soon split again and Leo was sent on to Dachau. Later, Henry was waiting in line for a train transport to go to some other camp when he overheard German soldiers talking about one of the other lines, destined for Dachau. Knowing his brother was in Dachau, Henry jumped to the other line when the guards looked away, hoping to reconnect with his brother.

By the time Henry arrived at Dachau, he was sick with typhus. Leo was in good health because he had a good job working on a locomotive. Leo helped bring Henry back to better health. At the end of the war, Henry and Leo were liberated at Dachau.

Abram and Eli, along with approximately 400 others, were sent to a camp which was set up in a small village called Pocking in Bavaria, near the border of Austria, where the Germans were building an airfield. They experienced the worst conditions yet: they were given very little food and slept on the floor of the prisoners' barracks. "Every morning, they rounded up the prisoners to walk out to the airfield about three kilometers away," Eli recounts. "One day, on the way to the airfield, Abram told me, 'Eli, I can't do it anymore. I'm ready to die.' I said to him, 'You're not killing yourself. You're not going to do the Germans any favors. As long as I'm alive, you're not killing yourself.' Abram didn't answer and I wondered how I would keep that promise.

"The next morning, I hid under the barracks. They always needed people to work in the camp. After the mechanics left, I helped to bury corpses. So I became a gravedigger. We filled carts with eight to ten dead bodies and moved them to the spot marked for burials. When I was a boy, I was scared to go near a house where someone had died. Now I was lifting corpses with my own hands. The prisoners were dying from malnutrition, dehydration, and typhus. We were all so weak."

He continues, "Toward the end of the war, the guards who watched over us in the camps were not the young soldiers you would have seen at the beginning of the war. They sent the young and healthy soldiers to the front lines. Now we were guarded by older German men who maybe weren't even soldiers. They didn't really know how many prisoners they had or who they were. That's why it was easier for me to hide."

Eli's determination kept his brother and him alive. "While carting the corpses to the burial sites, I would find cigarette butts on the street. I would collect the cigarette butts and make cigarettes out of about three butts. I could trade my cigarettes for extra soup or a carrot or a potato. Also, there were women who saw us on the street and they might take pity on us and offer us some food. I shared the extra food with Abram, and he regained his strength and will to live."

Finally, freedom! "We were in Pocking for six weeks. During that time, two hundred of the four hundred people died. We hoped the war was going to end soon. We heard rumors that the Americans were very close. One morning, we woke up and the guards had fled. We were able to just walk right out of the camp.

"A priest approached Abram, three other men, and me as we walked away from the camp. He took us to his house, let us bathe, and gave us clean clothes, food, and beds. He told us we could stay as long as we wanted to.

"There were two priests living in that house. The guy who approached us was a very nice guy but the other priest was not a nice guy. We thought he was an anti-Semite. But the priests were very afraid of the Russian prisoners of war who were now also getting released. The priests knew that the Russians would be seeking vengeance against Germans and were hopeful that by taking us in, we might be able to help protect them. Later we got sick from typhus and the priests brought us cabbage to help cure us, but in the process of helping us, they got sick and one died."

Many Jews stayed in Germany, either because they couldn't get visas to other countries, or because they wanted to stay in Germany, where they were helped by the United States government. In the years immediately following the end of the war, Israel was not yet a country so it wasn't an option for the survivors. While in Germany, Eli and Abram found their brothers, Leo and Henry, as well as their sister Fela, who escaped from a camp and was taken in by a sympathetic family, thanks to her blond hair and blue eyes, which allowed her to pass for a Christian. The five siblings planned to move to the United States and applied for visas.

Israel became a recognized country in 1948, creating a new opportunity for the survivors to leave Germany. Eli emigrated to Israel in 1949 while waiting for his US visa. While there, he met his wife in the factory where he worked. They were married in Israel in 1955. They had two children there: Ira, born in 1957, and Jacob, who was born in 1959 but died in infancy.

In 1960, Eli and his family sailed to America, where they rented an apartment in Brooklyn's East New York neighborhood. Another son, Myron, was born in 1961. The family moved to a bigger house in Canarsie, Brooklyn, where Eli could live within just a few miles of his three brothers. Sister Fela lived in New Jersey. Eli's first job in the US was machining steel for the first 747s. In 1971, he joined Abram's knitting mill business, which made sweaters. Eli fixed and maintained the Jacquard looms.

The five Rosmarin siblings who survived the war lived well into their eighties in the United States. Henry Rosmarin passed away in 2009 at the age of 92. Fela died in 2009 at the age of 89. Leo died in 2005 at the age of 83. Abram died in 2002 at the age of 84. Of the five, only Eli is still living. In 2010, he turned 87. Collectively, the five siblings raised 10 children and had 20 grandchildren.

Eli's youngest son, Myron, says, "The way my father and his brothers looked out for each other in the camps had a huge impact on my cousins, my brother, and me. Their courage made it possible for five kids from one family to survive when the odds were something like four out five family members of Jewish families perished. All these years later, we're still in awe of their tenacity and toughness. They continually demonstrated this survival sense throughout the remainder of their lives, perhaps none more so than Leo, who battled heart disease and multiple heart surgeries for almost thirty years. On several occasions when Leo's heart condition put him close to the brink, he battled back to rejoin his loving family. That's the stuff. They all had it."

POWER PRACTICE:

On Yom Hashoah, also known as Holocaust Remembrance Day, Jews commemorate the lives and heroism of those who died in the Holocaust, as well as the incredible strength and bravery of the survivors.

You may wish to create a similar day on which to commemorate the bravery of any group of persecuted people, such as those who experienced horrific ethnic cleansing efforts in the Balkans, or the genocides in Rwanda and Darfur. It is important to learn from history and to channel our collective courage to oppose such atrocities.

CRASH: DAD'S COURAGEOUS JOURNEY TO BUILD A NEW LIFE FOR HIS FAMILY

Start by doing what's necessary; then do what's possible; and suddenly you are doing the impossible.

—St. Francis of Assisi

Days after an automobile accident took the life of his wife and left his young sons seriously injured, Dwight Alexander made a decision: hope would follow the tragedy. Despite the death of his wife and the life-changing injuries to his sons, Dwight struggled to survive and to help his family thrive.

Under desperate circumstances, Dwight wanted the pain to go away. But in order to heal, he knew he had to go on. An inspiration for his two sons, his story speaks of the resilience of the human spirit.

"If Dwight Alexander has one message, it is this: Never give up."

The Sulphur Springs, Texas, father of five says, "You have no choice. It's a scary thing to be a dad and suddenly thrown into an emotional corner that you never expected to be in. You learn how to cry, to shed tears with your children, and to pick yourself up and show them that you can build a new life."

It was July 1999. Dwight Alexander was away on a business trip in Oklahoma. His two sons, Colin, 11, and Grant, 15 at the time, were riding in the car with their mom when another car raced through a stop sign. The boys' mother and Dwight's wife, Tina, was killed instantly. The brothers were rushed by helicopter to two separate hospitals where they would teeter on the brink of death for months.

"In one second, with one person's failure to stop at a stop sign, our lives were changed forever," Dwight says. He was determined that his sons would recover from their serious injuries and that God would make his family whole again.

Grant sustained a traumatic brain injury. Doctors said he would never walk or talk again. Colin was in a coma. Dwight spent months racing back and forth between the hospitals—and grieving the death of his wife. It took 15 months for Grant to say his first word. He has spent most of the intervening years in a wheelchair, but now he can walk.

Today, Grant is 25. He talks with a slur and works with Goodwill Industries. Colin is fully recovered and is a freshman in college, studying journalism and hoping to one day be an ESPN news anchor.

"People gave me books trying to give me advice to get through," Dwight remembers. "But they were all written by doctors and therapists. I was looking for a real person to come into my life who had survived something like this, who could show me there was hope."

This person soon appeared at the hospital. Her name was Michelle Thompson. A mom of three teens, she was a member of the same church that the Alexander family attended. Her husband had been killed in a motorcycle accident. Coincidentally, Tina Alexander had gone over to Michelle's house the night before her own death to help Michelle with some other members of the church.

"Three days after the accident, Grant was scheduled for brain surgery and I was feeling so alone," Dwight says. "I remember walking out of the room and through these doors, and there were about seven people from my church. There was Michelle. She was a good friend, the one person in the group who could understand the loss I was feeling. She was there for me, always."

In September 2001, two years following the accident, Michelle and Dwight were married, creating a blended family they affectionately dub "the modern-day Brady family." In the den of their home hang three pictures: portraits of the Dwight and Tina Alexander family, the David and Michelle Thompson family, and the new Dwight and Michelle Thompson and Alexander family.

Recently, Dwight authored a self-published book, *Through These Doors, A True Inspirational Story of a Family of Faith in Crisis*. The book is an account of the ordeal his family endured, focusing on how the grace of God moved through their lives to give them strength and to help them survive and triumph. Dwight travels the country to speak to grief groups and others who need inspiration. His purpose is to motivate others to face daily challenges, encouraging them to find the positive in every event of life.

POWER PRACTICE
Facing Crisis with Courage
Through his journey, Dwight Alexander learned the hard way how to cope with loss and endure the struggle to help his sons recover. He offers this advice:

- *You have to realize and then accept that you are single again, that you have to take on many of the roles that the "mom" used to do. It's hard because you find yourself at first feeling totally inadequate at the emotional stuff.*

- *You also have to realize that your child's livelihood depends on you and only you. That can be frightening, overwhelming.*

- *When someone you love is ill, you can't take no for an answer. They may tell you your loved one will never get well, but you can't believe that. You have to keep trying and believing it will be OK.*

- *Focus on the positive.*

- *Take one day at a time.*

- *Live for the moment. Not yesterday, not tomorrow.*

- *If your loved one has a brain injury, there is no immediate fix. Know it will be a long haul.*

- *Never give up. Don't quit.*

SEALS OF COURAGE: AGAINST ALL ODDS, NAVAL OFFICER STANDS UP TO TALIBAN TO SAVE HIS MEN

Courage is grace under pressure.

—*Ernest Hemingway*

Michael Murphy and Marcus Luttrell were best friends since the days they met in San Diego training to become Navy SEALs. But on a fateful day during a fierce battle with Taliban fighters in the mountains of eastern Afghanistan, Lt. Murphy lost his life when he broke his cover and stepped out into a field to try to make a rescue call on his cell phone.

In the years that followed, the story of Operation Red Wings and Lt. Murphy's extraordinary bravery and heroism made international headlines after Murphy, leader of the reconnaissance squad from Navy SEAL

Team 10, posthumously received the Congressional Medal of Honor for his heroic actions on June 28, 2005.

Michael was the first recipient of the nation's highest military honor as a result of US involvement in Afghanistan. He was also the first naval officer to earn the medal since the Vietnam War, and the first SEAL to be honored posthumously.

The recognition of Michael Murphy's gallantry is the final chapter of a story in which two brave young men and their four-man team displayed remarkable military heroism in the wake of 9/11. In fact, they dedicated their mission in Afghanistan to fallen firemen in New York City. Their mission was to help scout for Osama bin Laden, who was believed to be nearby.

But when they arrived in the village, they stumbled on some goat herders. They chose not to kill them. Torn between considerations of morality and their survival instincts, they chose to spare the three Afghans' lives. About an hour later, the Taliban launched an attack that claimed nearly a hundred of their own men and the lives of all the SEALs except Luttrell, who was left wounded.

Not long after that, the Taliban shot down an American rescue helicopter, killing all 16 men on board. Luttrell is sure that the three Afghans they let go turned around and betrayed the SEALs. Luttrell describes the encounter in his book, *Lone Survivor.*

Their story made national news in the US. Watching Michael Murphy's parents, and seeing Marcus at their side being interviewed by Matt Lauer, viewers couldn't help but be overwhelmed by compassion and awe at young men with such guts, passion, and commitment. And few viewers would be untouched by the sight of parents so proud of their fallen son, and by the thought of what life must be like for Marcus, the lone survivor.

A book that tells Michael Murphy's story, titled *SEAL of Honor: Operation Red Wings and the Life of Lt. Michael P. Murphy, USN*, is now in bookstores. And in reading *Lone Survivor*, anyone who has survived war, whether a literal war of nations or an abusive relationship, an attack of cancer, or a natural disaster, will be inspired by the gallantry and courage these two young men exhibited.

Early in his book, Marcus Luttrell quotes a mantra that Navy SEALs share with all survivors: "I will never quit. I persevere and thrive on adversity. I will get back up, every time. I will draw on every remaining ounce of strength to protect my teammates and to accomplish our mission. I am never out of fight."

POWER PRACTICE

If you are looking to be inspired, we recommend the accounts of bravery and heroism portrayed in these books: SEAL of Honor: Operation Red Wings and the

Life of Lt. Michael P. Murphy, USN, *by Gary Williams, and* Lone Survivor: The Eyewitness Account of Operation Redwing and the Lost Heroes of SEAL Team 10, *by Marcus Luttrell.*

CHAPTER NINE
THE COURAGE TO MAKE A DIFFERENCE

He who has a why to live can bear almost any how.

—*Friedrich Nietzsche*

We all know or hear about people who have been confronted with tragedy and vow to make their suffering matter and make a difference in the world.

We hear, "I don't want this to happen to another family, for anyone else to have to go through what I have experienced," and we are so grateful that these survivors are determined to put their spirit and passions out there to help others.

Some of those we interviewed never asked to become heroes or activists. They were placed in that position after tremendous suffering. But instead of crawling under the sheets, they moved through their fears to help others.

The power to transform your life and your fear into action is much closer than we realize.

MAKING HIS OWN KIND OF MUSIC:
BLIND HAITIAN VIOLINIST SURVIVED
EARTHQUAKE WITH RESOLVE TO GIVE GIFT OF
MUSIC TO CHILDREN

Pain is temporary. It may last a minute, or an hour, or a day, or a year, but eventually it will subside and something else will take its place. If I quit, however, it lasts forever.

—Lance Armstrong

When the earthquake ripped through his Port-au-Prince music school on January 12, 2010, killing his pregnant wife and trapping him under rubble for almost 20 hours, Romel Joseph did not expect to survive.

But somewhere in the depths of the rubble of what he thought would become his own grave, the blind Haitian violinist, Juilliard trained, began playing in his mind the strains of the Tchaikovsky concerto and all the violin concertos he had ever performed. After he was rescued, with his left hand crushed and with deep fractures in his left leg, Joseph sought medical treatment at the rehabilitation center of Miami's Jackson Memorial Hospital. He feared he would never walk again. But in March, just two months later, he defied the odds again, hop-walking across the stage at a benefit concert in Miami and raising his violin to play.

Joseph's remarkable rescue story caught the attention of Stevie Wonder and musicians across the globe, who have pledged to help him rebuild his New Victorian School in Turgeau, Port-au-Prince, Haiti, which he founded in 1992. With two keyboards donated by Stevie Wonder, he returned to the school on the day after Easter, in April 2010.

Romel Joseph was born almost completely blind and raised in poverty in Haiti. Today, the 50-year-old is considered his country's preeminent classical musician. His rescue from the debris of his school has drawn attention—and compassion—worldwide. Stevie Wonder donated keyboards to the New Victorian School, which Joseph founded in 1992.

It is the second time Joseph has had to completely rebuild his school and his dream to bring the music that has been his lifeline to young people. Ten years before the earthquake, a fire burned through the building and seriously damaged the school. Students returned to makeshift classrooms six weeks later, attending classes in late afternoon during the two years of reconstruction. This time it needs to be completely rebuilt. Musicians from primary schools to professional symphonies have pledged to help Joseph rebuild.

On April 3, 2010, Romel left the hospital he had called home since mid-January with pins in his left hand and rods jutting from his left leg. His daughter Victoria, 22, a music major at the University of Miami, and his son, Bradley, 17, were at his side. He still had months of rehabilitation to go, but he was a man on a mission to return to Haiti and reopen his school in tarp-covered classrooms.

But he has lost so much, and he says he knows much anguish lies ahead. His wife, Myslie, was seven months pregnant with a son. She was on the first floor of the school when the 7.0 earthquake ripped through that afternoon around 4:55 P.M., completely destroying the building shortly after the 300 students had left. Romel was one of the four people in the building who survived. Two others, including his wife, lost their lives.

Romel had just gone up to the third floor to deliver a phone message to a friend. While he was standing on the third floor balcony, the building began to tremble. Within seconds, it collapsed. Romel was trapped under the rubble of the school for 20 hours. His legs and feet were pinned under the concrete support beams of the fourth and fifth floors. The next morning, at about 11 A.M., he was freed from his "concrete tomb." Two days later, he was airlifted by the American Embassy to the Florida hospital.

"I thought I would never play music again, but there

was nothing I could do about it," he recalled. "When you're underground and don't know if you're going to come out alive, your hands are the least of your worries."

He estimates it will take several years to rebuild the school, but it will operate in a temporary shelter until then. Upon his return, he had already raised about half of the $35,000 he needs to operate the school in the temporary shelter.

Romel is no stranger to adversity—he has spent much of his life overcoming it. Born into poverty in the small town of Gros Morne in central Haiti, he lost his eyesight to an infection that could have been treated if his family had had money. He was sent to a school for the handicapped in Port-au-Prince, where the nuns introduced him to the violin and piano. He practiced endlessly, won a scholarship to a music college in Cincinnati, and then a Fulbright scholarship to the elite Juilliard School in New York. He went on to achieve international renown and became an American citizen.

While at the rehab center, at his doctor's urging, Joseph picked up his violin. At first struggling to put his fingers on the strings and play single notes, he was soon entertaining fellow patients and the staff with some of his repertoire, including "My Favorite Things" from *The Sound of Music*. It is one of the songs he played in his mind while he was trapped in the rubble of the earthquake.

Joseph says the song was the inspiration that helped

him overcome his fears. He remembers how he sang to himself: "When the dog bites, when the bee stings, when I'm feeling sad, I simply remember my favorite things and then I don't feel so bad." He started thinking about his favorite thing—music—and kept himself sane throughout the ordeal by playing in his mind all the violin concertos he'd ever performed. "I used music, which is what I always do when I'm in trouble," he says.

Shortly after the earthquake, Romel left his rehab center to return to Haiti with his daughter to direct an operation to clear the rubble and rebuild the school. His goal was to be able to give scholarships to poor Haitian children who had been maimed and orphaned in the disaster. In an article in the *Miami Times* he said, "You never give up. You never stop. You have to keep going."

By late autumn, he hopes, he will be back to playing professionally. He is looking forward to being able to dance again, to travel and perform with Victoria, who plays viola, and Bradley, a pianist.

"I came to the hospital ninety-nine-point-nine percent dead," Joseph says. "I left eighty-five percent healed. I am so thankful for the emotional, psychological, physical, and financial support I received. We will forever be grateful to those who helped us continue our mission."

Donations to the school can be made through the Walenstein Musical Organization, Romel's nonprofit based in Miami. www.walensteinmusic.org.

POWER PRACTICE

Sometimes the way we can overcome our own fears is to know we are helping others. In giving of ourselves, we tap into a place inside us that is larger and more powerful than our fears. Romel Joseph spent 20 hours of terror playing music in his mind. We encourage you to pause for a moment and imagine listening to the sounds of children in Haiti who are filling their hearts and spirits with music and the hope it can bring for their future.

THE MOST VULNERABLE AMONG US: SAVING THE LIVES OF THOSE GIVING LIFE TO OTHERS

If you lose hope, somehow you lose the vitality that keeps life moving, you lose that courage to be, that quality that helps you go on in spite of it all. And so today I still have a dream.

—Martin Luther King Jr.

Did you know that two to three women die every day in the United States during or after childbirth and that half of those deaths are entirely preventable?

According to the World Health Organization, the US ranks behind more than 40 other countries in maternal death rates. The likelihood of a woman dying in childbirth in the United States is five times greater than in Greece, four times greater than in Germany, and three times greater than in Spain. Many experts believe the phenomenon is on the rise; in fact, a report found that the mortality rate of California women who die from causes directly related to pregnancy has nearly tripled in the last decade, making it more dangerous to give birth in California than in Kuwait or Bosnia. The California Department of Health, which commissioned the report by the California Maternal Quality Care Collaborative (CMQCC), has not yet publicly released it as of 2010.

Tatia Oden French, of Oakland, California, is one of those featured in the study. She completed her doctoral degree in June 2000, married, became pregnant, and was due to give birth in December 2001. In perfect health, Tatia was versed in the latest studies on maternal health and infant care. She wasn't planning to use disposable diapers after learning that they release toxic compounds; and she planned to feed her baby only organic, natural food. After following a method of natural childbirth she was determined to deliver her baby without the use of drugs.

Two weeks after her estimated due date, she was persuaded to go to the hospital, and after five hours of debate, she gave in to her doctor's insistence on inducing the birth.

Tatia's mother, Maddy Oden, went home to sleep but abruptly awoke at 4:00 A.M. She had a scary premonition that something was terribly wrong.

Tatia Oden French was 32 years old, in perfect health, and looking forward to a natural, unmedicated childbirth. There were no problems during the pregnancy.

According to her doctor's estimate, she was almost two weeks overdue. She was given the drug Cytotec (misoprostol) to induce her labor. The drug, which is not approved by the FDA for inducing labor, is for the treatment of ulcers. Ten hours after being administered Cytotec Tatia suffered serious complications, and an emergency C-section was performed because the baby was in distress.

When she arrived at the hospital, Tatia's mother, Maddy, had to fight her way into the labor and delivery section of the hospital. By the time she got to Tatia's room, it was deserted and the bed was gone, signifying a hasty move. "I don't remember feeling fear at that point," says this Queens, New York, native, who at the time worked for the City of Berkeley as an accounting office specialist. "It was more of a feeling that a force was propelling me forward. Something was wrong, and my objective was to find out what it was."

She remembers being completely disoriented, and not getting any information from anyone. Finally, she ran into Tatia's husband, J.B. French. He mumbled, "Tatia's gone." Maddy asked him, "Gone where?" And then it sank in. Maddy fell to the floor screaming and everything went black.

Then a voice inside her head instructed her to get up and find her daughter. She again wandered through the empty corridors until she found her way to the operating room. The medical staff at this highly respected medical institution was sequestered in a meeting to make sure they got their story straight. Maddy finally located the operating room where her daughter's and granddaughter's bodies lay. Maddy closed Tatia's eyes and summoned the family. Surrounding Tatia and her baby, Zorah Allie Mae French, family members said a prayer and then said their goodbyes.

Maddy tried to find out what happened. She learned that the drug had caused an amniotic fluid embolism (AFE) in her daughter's lungs, and the hyperstimulation of the maternal uterus had killed the baby. Maddy asked the doctor to promise her that she would never again prescribe that drug. "The doctor said, 'I can't promise that,' " Maddy remembers, and at that moment she knew she had to do something to prevent this from happening to other women.

Maddy had to dig deep inside herself in order to keep going, and she found that the only way to honor her daughter and granddaughter was to work hard at making a difference in the lives of *all* women who are pregnant. Maddy has since become a certified doula herself, working as a volunteer at San Francisco General Hospital on the labor and delivery floor and as a pro bono doula throughout the Bay Area.

She established a nonprofit foundation, The Tatia Oden French Memorial Foundation (www.tatia.org), to raise awareness about the risks of induced labor and cesarean sections, and about the issues of informed consent, off-label use of drugs, and maternal mortality. The foundation, formed in March 2003, is dedicated to empowering women around the issues of childbirth and pregnancy. It provides all women of childbearing age complete information about medical interventions and the drugs that are administered during childbirth, so women may be able to make fully informed decisions regarding the birth of their children.

Maddy is encouraged that she is on the front lines, partnering with other organizations to further the public's knowledge about this life-and-death issue. She is involved in the Coalition for Improving Maternity Services (CIMS). Amnesty International has released a report titled "Deadly Delivery" about the crisis of maternal health in the US. In addition, a documentary film by Christy Turlington Burns, titled *No Woman, No Cry,* has been released, telling the powerful personal stories of women in Bangladesh, Guatemala, Tanzania, and the United States whose lives lie in the balance of the safe motherhood movement.

Maddy is hopeful that these movements will make a difference. Her goals are impressive: stopping the use of the drug Cytotec for inducing labor, reducing the maternal mortality rate in the US, and empowering women to be fully informed of all their choices when they give their consent to a procedure or intervention during labor and delivery.

We salute the courage of her deep convictions, and

her belief that no one should ever have to suffer the loss of a daughter as she did. "Don't be afraid of not making a difference when you want to change something," she advises. "You've got nothing to lose."

POWER PRACTICE

When you think, I can't go on, because the absolute worst thing has happened to me, it is important to latch on to anything we can think of to keep going.

If you are depressed, you can start a new morning ritual, or make a weekly appointment with a good friend. What often works is volunteering for a cause you feel strongly about. You may find solace being around others who can understand your feelings. Plus, many studies have shown the connection between volunteering and lower rates of depression. Start by joining the local branch of an organization tackling issues that are meaningful to you. It will help give you the courage to go on, and to make a difference in the world.

SAVING GRACES: AFTER FIGHTING OVARIAN CANCER, SHE'S HELPING EDUCATE WOMEN, THEIR DOCTORS, AND MEN ABOUT THE SILENT SYMPTOMS OF THIS MOST DEADLY OF DISEASES

Have courage for the great sorrows of life, and patience for the small ones. When you have laboriously accomplished your daily tasks, go to sleep in peace. God is awake.

—Victor Hugo

When Susan Roman, a Buffalo Grove, Illinois, mom of two, got the diagnosis of stage III ovarian cancer in August 2009, she drew on her innately strong will and resourcefulness to manage the next months of treatment step by step. She was determined not to miss a beat.

The truth is, Susan was pretty shaken but determined to stay strong for her two children and her husband, Rick. It was her intention, as director of human resources at The Signature Room on the 95th floor of Chicago's John Hancock building, to keep business running smoothly and not to concern the 250 employees at that popular

221

Chicago eatery. To cope, she reached deep inside to access her strong faith. "The world seemed to be passing me by, going on as normal, but not for me," she recalls. "I realized I could be nervous and afraid, or I could skip that. So I turned all the fear into an opportunity to touch base spiritually, and I just prayed, 'Thy will be done.' "

Just a year and a half after her diagnosis, Susan, 53, is in remission. Together with her good friend Vallie Szymanski and her husband, Rick, she has launched a nonprofit called Ovarian Cancer Symptom Awareness (www.ovariancancersymptomawareness.org).

"We hope to save a life through educating women, their families, and their doctors on the silent symptoms of ovarian cancer," Susan says. "We intend to get the somewhat vague symptoms out into the public so women will begin to pay more attention to what is going on in their bodies and have more open communication with their doctors about the symptoms they feel."

For years, family and friends have called Susan Roman "Goose." It's a well-deserved compliment—she's the one who keeps the flock together in V formation: her community of family, friends, and supporters. Two years before her own cancer fallout, her husband, Rick, was injured in a serious motorcycle accident. Susan was called on to smile and grit her teeth when doctors announced that Rick had sustained a traumatic brain injury. "That's when I learned about courage and digging down deep," she recalls. Thankfully, and through the grace of the couple's strong faith, Rick recovered fully.

It is with precise intention that the inspiring symbol of a goose, which never leaves one of its kind behind, is the logo and working metaphor for Ovarian Cancer Symptom Awareness (OCSA). These incredibly gifted navigators are strong-willed and resourceful. Geese always forge ahead with confidence and bravery, instinctively knowing how to go the long distance to wherever they are headed.

Like the goose, Susan is determined that no woman's journey through ovarian cancer should ever be a solo one. The foundation is committed to carrying other women, rising together to help create awareness of this dreadful disease.

For Susan, her diagnosis was a watershed moment. Ovarian cancer had claimed the life of her mother in 1976. "In those very different times, my mother's doctors barely communicated with her, their patient," Susan recalls. She was only 19 at the time. "Instead, they discussed her condition and treatment with my father, assigning him the task to decide what to tell her and what to hold back. My mom died in April 1976—a mere three months after her diagnosis and one day after her fifty-second birthday. I vividly recall the devastating effect my mom's illness and death had on me—on all my family."

Susan immediately became passionate about the cause

and made it her practice to be vigilant about her own health care. But like many women, she dismissed vague symptoms as stress, keeping her focus on the needs of her family and her job. Working with a personal trainer one day, she felt a lump in her stomach. She raced to the doctor, and a CT scan confirmed the worst. A diagnosis, not a prognosis, stage III means the cancer has spread from the ovaries and pelvic organs into the upper abdomen or lymph nodes. In Susan's case, the cancer had spread to her appendix, fallopian tube, and omentum (one of the folds of the peritoneum that connects the stomach to other abdominal organs). Following a radical hysterectomy and about a month of recovery, she embarked on a course of six chemotherapy treatments.

"Since my diagnosis, I have asked myself repeatedly what symptom I missed. Thinking back, I now suspect weight gain in my upper abdominal area to be the most significant symptom I overlooked. I had started working out with a personal trainer and actually believed I was developing abdominal muscles for the first time since the births of my two children. I held that happy thought until I felt a lump.

"This discovery set in motion a visit with my primary care physician, a CT scan, appointments with a gyne-cologic oncologist and a gynecologic surgeon, and, ulti-mately, led to a diagnosis of stage III ovarian cancer."

From the start, Susan was determined to stay tough for

her daughter Angela, 27, and her son Dominic, 22. "My attitude was to get through the chemo and everything and stay close-mouthed, not to worry anyone else." But like the geese, Susan's friends rallied to her side to carry and support her through the months of treatment. Her friend Vallie, she says, pledged to do something that would be longer lasting. The seed for the foundation was planted.

Susan began learning as much as she could about ovarian cancer. She found out that many women, including herself, are often diagnosed with ovarian cancer when it is already at an advanced stage. This can be attributed to a lack of early-detection technologies and a host of symptoms that can be mistaken for many other ailments and diseases. By learning more about risk factors and maintaining regular consultations with doctors, women have their best chance of early detection.

"When I heard my diagnosis, I felt scared and sorry for myself, asking *Why me?* I stayed stuck in that mode until a successful surgery and hours in prayer acted as a catalyst to shift my thinking to *Why not me?* Gradually, with more recovery time and processing, I moved on to realize I may be, in fact, just the woman to take on the challenge of promoting awareness of the symptoms of ovarian cancer: I belong to a seemingly boundless support system of family and friends; I possess a history of firsthand experience with ovarian cancer; and, consequently, I now know many medical professionals and their related organizations, assuring invaluable resources to guide me. Feeling energized and determined to help as many women as I can to detect ovarian cancer *early*, I proceeded to take the necessary action to create Ovarian Cancer Symptom Awareness."

Just months into the launching of the nonprofit, Susan's restaurateur family and the foundation have a smorgasbord of programs lined up to make a difference. "We want to create an awareness that does not exist," she says. "We want there to be resources like walk-in CT scans and less expensive CA-125 blood tests available to women. Our goal is simple; we want to save at least one life."

POWER PRACTICE

There is something you can do to help fight ovarian cancer. If it is detected in its earliest stages, the five-year survival rate is more than 93 percent. Proper education about the symptoms and signs can make a huge difference. One thing you can do is help spread the word. Recent research suggests that four symptoms in particular—bloating, pelvic or abdominal pain, difficulty eating or feeling full quickly, and urinary urgency—may be associated with ovarian cancer. Don't stay silent.

FIVE TIPS FOR PUTTING YOUR PASSIONS OUT THERE

Many people, like Susan Roman, who have survived the blow of cancer or significant illness pick themselves up off the pavement to become champions and crusaders in the war against their disease and in an attempt to bring their message to finding a cure.

As one of the lucky ones who can call herself a survivor of lung cancer, Bonnie Addario of San Carlos, California, became a tireless crusader to get the world to focus on this number one cancer killer, which has long been swept under the rug as the "stigma cancer." She founded the Bonnie J. Addario Lung Cancer Foundation (www.thelungcancerfoundation.org) to raise awareness to the urgency of finding a cure for lung cancer.

Here she offers five tips for those who want to transform adversity into making a difference:

1. Don't waste any more time putting off going after your dreams because you are facing a roadblock. Even in the face of adversity, you need to keep moving toward what you want in your life. I realized that it isn't just having

cancer—it is an experience that threatens your life and all the dreams you had for it. One thing you quickly discover is that time is of the essence. You have to go after your dreams now.

2. Ask yourself who you can help. Once you've experienced cancer or something really challenging in your life, you can no longer naively think you are isolated from such things, or that they only happen to other people. Look around for the people that may need your help. Explore what you can do to make a positive difference in their lives.

3. Be grateful. Wake up each day thrilled with how wonderful it is to have another one. Embrace and enjoy all the things in your life you didn't see before the adversity set in.

4. Be the change you want to see in the world. There are no more excuses. Do what matters to you and don't worry what anyone else thinks. If you feel there is a cause you want to support, go do it.

5. Ask for guidance. Don't be afraid to reach

out and ask others to help you if you really are intent on making a difference in the world. Sometimes we stay stuck in our tracks because we are overwhelmed and afraid we will fail. Don't be afraid of connecting with the people who can help you.

COURAGE UNDER FIRE: NAVY OFFICER AND MOM SUMMONS THE COURAGE TO BE A GUARDIAN ANGEL TO WOUNDED MILITARY PERSONNEL

Nobody escapes being wounded. We all are wounded people, whether physically, emotionally, mentally, or spiritually. The main question is not "How can we hide our wounds?" so we don't have to be embarrassed, but "How can we put our woundedness in the service of others?"

—Henri Nouwen

When former Lieutenant Commander Heidi Kraft's twin son and daughter were 15 months old, she was deployed to Iraq. An active duty Navy clinical psychologist with a Marine Corps surgical company, Heidi's job was to uncover the wounds of war that a surgeon would never see. She put away thoughts of her children back home, acclimated to the sound of incoming rockets, and learned how to listen to the most traumatic stories a war zone has to offer.

Now living at home in San Diego with her elementary school-aged twins, Brian and Megan, and her husband, Mike, Heidi has transformed her own wounds from the war to become a source of healing for other military men and women. Through her story, we understand better the courage it takes to be on the front lines of combat in Iraq, but also the bravery one must muster to return to a life that is never quite "normal" again. With great candor and intimate insight, Heidi shares how she had to confront her own trauma and how terrifying it was to return home with the ghosts of war haunting her psyche.

Trained to be stoic and strong, Heidi Kraft spent seven months in 2004 at a remote air base in western Iraq, holding the hands of dying soldiers and listening and comforting them as they wept. On one particularly difficult day, she had to tell a room full of stunned Marines in blood-soaked uniforms that their comrade, whom they had tried to save, had just died of his wounds.

She will never forget the lessons she learned on the front lines of the war during her service as a member of the SST (Shock Stabilization Team) at a hospital in Al Asad, Iraq. Though she witnessed countless deaths, one Marine, Corporal Jason Dunham, stuck with her. His death changed her life and was the inspiration for her 2007 book, *Rule Number Two: Lessons I Learned in a Combat Hospital* (www.rulenumbertwo.com).

Heidi held Jason's hand after he was brought in with severe head trauma, attempting to comfort him in what she believed would be his final moments. At the sound of

Heidi's voice, the injured combatant squeezed her hand, proving there was life and lucidity within his fractured body. She held that Marine's hand until he was able to be evacuated from Iraq to Bethesda, Maryland, where he was met by his parents. He died shortly after.

Ten days after her team had treated Corporal Dunham, she was filing out of Mass when she found the chief of her team waiting for her. He informed her that Jason had just died. "Bethesda called this morning," he told her. "They know we've been following his progress. I wanted you to hear first."

Nearly a week later, late one evening, a soldier came in to give her some information about Dunham. "Ma'am, it appears that Corporal Dunham threw himself on a grenade. He placed his helmet over a live grenade and tucked it under his body, to save his men."

Heidi forged a close bond with Deb Dunham, Jason's mother, and even accompanied the Dunhams to the White House in January 2007 as they accepted their son's Congressional Medal of Honor from President Bush. In 2009, Heidi again accompanied Jason's family when the Navy named a ship in his honor.

For Dunham, Heidi was there when his mom couldn't be, a guardian angel providing comfort and aid for many children of our country. Her book is dedicated to Corporal Dunham's mom, "the mother of a hero," and her husband, Mike.

In an excerpt from her book, she describes more experiences of life on the front lines:

> After the first half hour, I allowed myself to lean my head back, focusing on the muscles in my shoulders, which felt like rubber bands under tension. Had it only been twelve hours since that mass casualty? I scrunched my eyes shut, willing the tears to stay inside. Distracted by my trepidation about this convoy, I had not allowed myself time to think about Corporal Dunham. Or about that young lance corporal I had met early in the day as he recovered from surgery on our ward. I remembered the tattoos on his arms. One said USMC. And one, he told me, used to say SEMPER FI. After that day's car bomb had taken out most of his forearm, only the S and the E remained. I remembered his tears and the way he swiped mercilessly at them. He felt fear. He felt shame that far outweighed the fear. He went on to explain that he had been in Iraq almost two months. This injury would earn him his third Purple Heart. He told me he was afraid his luck was about to run out. He was ashamed to feel afraid.
>
> I remembered struggling to form the words that would normalize this nineteen-year-old

man's experience. And using a therapeutic technique I made up as I went along, I consciously decided to take another path instead. I told him there was nothing normal about three Purple Hearts in two months. I told him there were no feelings that were usual for people in that situation. I told him he was going home. He laid his head on his pillow and sobbed without making a sound. I sat with him a long time. I thought of my Brian, only seventeen months old. I pictured myself lying in bed when the phone rang in the darkness. I physically experienced that sick, sinking sensation that must invade every mother's heart the moment she hears a shrill ring fracture the night. I thought of that lance corporal's mother. I thought of Corporal Dunham's mother. I bit my lip hard and tasted blood.

For months after returning from Iraq, Heidi endured her nightmares of anger, sadness, and guilt about having had to leave her young children. "The process of becoming a mom and wife again was painfully slow and very scary. I realized that the only way I was going to become whole again was to confront what happened there, to share my story and expose the trauma."

In healing her own wounds, Heidi experienced firsthand that it takes great courage and internal strength to retrace a challenging experience in order to alchemically transform it into the life force to help others.

"I had to give myself a break and give myself permission to take care of myself and honor all I was feeling," Heidi recalls. "I also had to reach out to the people who cared about me for social support. I went back to the gym and exercised a lot and I decided to write a book for me, to experience my feelings, never intending for it to be published or to be read by anyone else."

Today, back in San Diego after nine years of active duty in the Navy, Heidi continues to work to change the way the military takes care of its wounded—specifically those fractured emotionally by the constant barrage on their physical health and the trauma of combat. As a consultant to both the Navy's and Marine Corps' combat stress control programs, she provides psychological treatment and care for active duty patients diagnosed with posttraumatic stress disorder, and she shares, through public speaking, relevant and timely messages of growth and healing after combat trauma, a topic that is receiving increasing public interest.

The title of her book comes from an episode in the first season of the television series *M*A*S*H*, "Sometimes You Hear the Bullet." In this 1973 episode, Hawkeye, a surgeon, realizes he cannot save a youthful Marine. Henry says to Hawkeye, "In war, rule number one is that young men die. And rule number two is that doctors cannot change rule number one."

Heidi says, "My own experience with the trauma taught me that we heal by reaching out and connecting to others who have gone through it too. It's easier to try to run away. But the courage comes from moving through the painful experience and struggling to heal."

POWER PRACTICE

Stop for a moment and ask yourself who in your life has helped you through difficult times. Not a person who has dispensed advice, or told you to just buck up, have courage, and get through it. Rather, a person who has shared his or her pain and reached back to hold your hand through yours. Take a moment to be grateful for those who have stayed with you during times of uncertainty. And remember, someday it may be your turn to stand at someone's side during moments when they feel powerless.

PROFILES IN COURAGE

The Profile in Courage Award, named for John F. Kennedy's 1957 Pulitzer prize-winning book *Profiles in Courage*, was created in 1989 by members of President Kennedy's family to honor him by recognizing and celebrating the quality of political courage that he admired most. The Profile in Courage Award seeks to make Americans aware of the conscientious and courageous acts of their public servants, and to encourage elected officials to choose principles over partisanship—to do what is right, rather than what is expedient.

Profile in Courage Award Recipients
Carl Elliott Sr. (1990)
Charles Weltner (1991)
Lowell Weicker Jr. (1992)
James Florio (1993)
Henry Gonzalez (1994)
Michael Synar (1995)
Corkin Cherubini (1996)

Charles Price (1997)
Nickolas Murnion (1998)
Peacemakers of Northern Ireland (1998)
Russell Feingold (1999)
John McCain (1999)
Hilda Solis (2000)
Gerald Ford (2001)
John Lewis (2001)
Kofi Annan (2002)
Dean Koldenhoven (2002)
Public Servants of September 11 (2002)
Roy Barnes (2003)
David Beasley (2003)
Dan Ponder Jr. (2003)
Paul Muegge (2004)
Sima Samar (2004)
Cindy Watson (2004)
Joseph Darby (2005)
Shirley Franklin (2005)
Bill Ratliff (2005)
Viktor Yushchenko (2005)
Alberto Mora (2006)
John Murtha (2006)
Doris Voitier (2007)
Bill White (2007)
Debra Bowen (2008)
Jennifer Brunner (2008)

William Winter (2008)
Edward M. Kennedy (2009)
Sheila Bair (2009)
Brooksley Born (2009)
Leymah Gbowee and the Women of Liberia (2009)

CHAPTER TEN

JUST TRY IT

Don't wait for your ship to come in. Row out to meet it.

—Author unknown

"Just do it" is one of the most famous and recognized quotes in advertising history, created by the Nike Corporation for its Reebok line of athletic footwear. It captures the very essence of an athlete's motivation.

But aren't we all athletes of sorts in our own life, training and practicing to be our personal best? Sometimes we fall. Sometimes we're exhausted and just don't feel like trying. And sometimes we are afraid we just can't do it.

The whole concept of "just do it," or "just try it," is not merely a marketing gimmick. It is the power source that propels us to tap into our courage and try something new. When we do, we reach a tipping point where we turn from thinking and fretting about something to doing it and proving it.

Introducing this concept into our lives sets a new standard for how we live. Imagine what your life would be like if you celebrated the "just do it" spirit in your life. Think about how that could help you face down and overcome so many obstacles in your life.

How do you overcome the fears that prevent you from moving forward? How do you start a new business when you are worried about finances? How do you embrace love again when your track record in that category hasn't been so great? How do you take your hopes and dreams and act on them?

Well, the bottom line is, if you don't "just do it," your fear of failure is certainly going to become a fear of success. And if we fear the success that could happen, well then, it's not likely to manifest itself.

ACHIEVING YOUR DREAMS: YOUNGEST PERSON TO CIRCUMNAVIGATE THE GLOBE SOLO THINKS TAKING RISKS IS THE EASY PART

It is not because things are difficult that we do not dare; it is because we do not dare that they are difficult.

—Seneca

Brian ("B.J.") Caldwell, 34, began to dream of circumnavigating the globe while spending high school summer breaks providing yacht deliveries, a job that contributed to his sailing over 10,000 miles while still in his teens. He formulated a plan to set sail exactly 100 years after Joshua Slocum set off on the first successful solo sail around the world in 1895, and on June 1, 1995, B.J. departed on his own quest. Sixteen months and 27,000 miles later, he set a record as the youngest solo circumnavigator in history.

Fifteen years later, B.J. is relaxed as he describes why he was apprehensive before departing land. "I was just very anxious to finally get under way, as I'd been hoping to leave since age fifteen and had already circumnavigated countless times in my mind. In my case, reaching the start was by far the biggest obstacle versus those encountered along the geographical lap around the planet."

For the rest of us, the thought of being pummeled by extreme waves in an open ocean in a small boat might be the daunting part!

B.J, who divides his time between France, racing aboard his Open 650 race boat; Hawaii, where he has an international yacht delivery business; and Australia, where he plans to attempt to win the 630-nautical-mile Sydney to Hobart Race (widely considered one of the most difficult in the world) a second time, describes how he dealt with fear during his solo voyage, and gives us all a lesson in living life with true power and courage.

According to this competitor, the scariest part of a solo voyage is that "the trip, for the most part, is destined for success or failure *before* it physically begins, during the big preliminary conceptual decisions such as routing, type of boat, budget, etcetera." B.J. Caldwell says, "Strategic decisions impact the results, and once decided upon and the launch button is pressed, those decisions can't be retracted." He adds, "One of the biggest obstacles I faced was paying the costs of the trip. I was terrified that this goal might turn out to be only a pipe dream."

B.J. was well prepared for the physical risks of his trip. While still in high school, he had sailed from Hawaii intending to circle the planet in less than one year. He changed his plans, visiting Samoa and Fiji in favor of a fast passage, and arrived in Port Vila, Vanuatu (formerly known as the New Hebrides) 34 days later, having covered 3,400 miles. His next stop was Cocos Keeling Islands in the Indian Ocean, and then 2,300 miles to Mauritius, where the weather deteriorated until he was capsized by trade winds. The impact bent his solar panels and dumped a foot of water in the bilge, ruining most of his provisions.

His next destination was Africa. Close to shore, the day before Thanksgiving, he barely avoided being run down by a tanker in the busy shipping route from the Arabian oil fields. Ten hours after he arrived, there were 30-foot seas along the 100-fathom line. B.J. describes his near miss with the tanker as the most dangerous moment of the voyage. "Just the sickening chance that something besides Mother Nature would stop me was impossible to comprehend," he says.

B.J. has an unusual response to fear. "The longer I've done this, the better accustomed I've become to understand what are productive levels of apprehension and at what point I believe it becomes detrimental." He says, "Generally, the worse it gets, the more I laugh. A little or, better yet, a lot of humor can combat fear far better than anything else. So I tell my crew in tough situations, 'You know it's getting pretty bad if I'm laughing hysterically.'"

His advice for those of us who daydream about pursuing our dreams? "It's often been said, but needs to be drummed into our minds until we really believe the words and what they mean: Never give up, don't take no for an answer, and remember above all that persistence and hard work will ultimately enable the means to make your goal materialize, usually just when you thought all hope was lost. I cannot emphasize enough the importance of persistence."

He continues, "You should also do it for the right reasons. A record pursuit might open professional doors later, but first and foremost, you need to do it because you love your pursuit and would rather do nothing else. If it's reached the point where achieving your dream has become your reason for living or a kind of personal religion, you are ready to not take no for an answer." To follow B.J.'s future adventures, you can find him at www.liquidflight.net.

POWER PRACTICE

If you've recently taken the plunge to pursue your dream of starting a new career, or writing a novel, or breaking a record, but you periodically become scared, here's something you can do: reflect back on your original motivation.

Why did you want to quit your job to start a new career

or a new business? What made you sacrifice hundreds of hours of your leisure time writing each page of your new novel?

Whatever has the power to compel your dream in the first place has the power to sustain it. Try channeling that anxious energy into constructive wisdom by writing down all the reasons that got you started in the race in the first place.

BREEDING SUCCESS:
LESSONS IN BECOMING A BIG DOG

It is not the mountain we conquer but ourselves.

—Edmund Hillary

Chuck it all, and start a magazine? Yes, it's been done, but in recent years when many established magazines are either folding or letting go of staff, it seems like a very daring thing to do. Over 10 years ago, the founders of Bark *magazine didn't worry about the future when they created a lifestyle magazine for people with dogs. In fact, they never had a business plan. But they did have gumption, passion, and courage.*

Originally founded in 1997 as an eight-page newsletter,

Bark evolved into an international publication that addresses the burgeoning issues faced by a new generation of dog owners. Today, the magazine has a circulation of 125,000 and is growing with each issue, in sharp contrast to other niche magazines.

Did the two founders, Cameron Woo and Claudia Kawczynska, have an extraordinary amount of bravery and confidence when they set out to fulfill their vision? In this story, Cameron lets us in on the lessons he's learned from following his bliss, facing the unknown, and finding his true path.

Cameron Woo, publisher of *Bark,* the award-winning Berkeley-based magazine that publishes a roster of acclaimed writers including Ann Patchett, Augusten Burroughs, Rick Bass, Amy Hempel, and Pulitzer Prize-winning poet Mary Oliver, does not think of himself as an entrepreneur. In fact, he says he's typically risk adverse and that his family encouraged stability and security.

He did choose a profession that fell outside the range of acceptable choices for his family—graphic design—but he decided to work in corporate settings, including AT&T, where he toiled in the corporate communications department early in his career before moving to the software company Autodesk as an art director. While at AT&T, he was asked to volunteer at a homeless shelter in San Francisco, where he soon joined the board of directors and served two years as its president. This was his first experience running an organization. Then, when he and his life partner, Claudia Kawczynska, got their first dog, Nell, they wanted to let her run leashless through the park; for this they needed to rally support from other dog owners.

He and Claudia organized Friends of César Chávez Park. Instead of fearing the fight with city hall, or park authorities, in 1996 Claudia and Cameron handed out about a thousand copies of a newsletter at the Berkeley Marina and left a few stacks at pet stores. *Bark* was born.

"We soon saw that there was an opportunity to make this a national magazine," Cameron remembers. "However, I had no training in magazine publishing, and had to learn an entirely new skill set from scratch."

Cameron describes the radical changes in his life. "I had gone from being part of an organizational setting where I had the support of three thousand people to a support system of two," he recalls. "I quickly learned that if I didn't do it, it didn't get done." He says that in contrast to a corporate setting, where you can hide for a day or even for your entire career, when you are on your own there is nowhere to hide.

He was not afraid of the financial consequences of failing. "I know people who have real problems—a good friend of mine has an eight-year old daughter with type 1 diabetes. Now that's serious. If our magazine failed, no one was going to get hurt; no one was going to die. The worst thing that will happen is we will have to close our doors." He continues, "I've never understood people's fear of failure. Some people are frozen in place by their need for security."

His advice for anyone who is considering starting a new business? "Build on a foundation that allows you to take that leap," he says, "and don't let anyone dissuade you from following your passion. Even if it fails, you will know that you gave it a shot, that you learned a lot, and you'll be able to say, Wow, I created something special."

And for all of us, he advises, "You can draw on inner courage by devoting yourself to doing something risky. Courage can be practiced in degrees—it doesn't have to be something huge that you do all at once. Carve out space to be challenged and courageous."

POWER PRACTICE
Sometimes we ascribe extraordinary talent or luck to people who achieve superstardom or fabulous wealth. Actually, in many cases, it has more to do with motivation and drive than with good fortune. Horatio Alger was a 19th-century American author who wrote "rags to riches" stories. This scenario, which has fueled so many success stories of the American Dream, is accessible to us even in recessionary times. All it takes is a positive attitude and the courage to make it happen.

A POSITIVE APPROACH TO COURAGE: SIMPLE SELF-HELP TECHNIQUES

In general, positive thinking promotes positive outcomes, and pessimism begets negativity.

Michele Kirk often preaches this basic message when working with parents and couples. She encourages her clients to notice one positive thing about their child or partner each day, comment on it, and then watch the results. She also encourages clients to begin noticing their own self-talk and to challenge the negative stories they often tell themselves.

TRY THIS:

To train yourself to start thinking more positively, say three positive self-statements out loud before you go to bed each night. Think about what you did well during the day at work, how you helped your children, a new friend you met, and so on.

Or create a positive affirmation, write it on a sticky note, and post it in your car, at your desk, or on your bathroom mirror so that you see it often. Say it out loud to yourself several times a day. In this way we can empower ourselves to break out of old negative labels that keep us stuck and are no longer helpful.

EXAMPLES OF POSITIVE AFFIRMATIONS:

- I know that I can handle all that comes my way.

- I am in control of my fears.

- Challenging my fears helps me grow and makes me stronger.

Michele Kirk is a marriage and family therapist in private practice in the San Francisco Bay Area. Visit her at www.michelekirk.com.

THE NUMBER ONE FEAR:
DON'T SUFFER IN SILENCE

According to most studies, people's number one fear is public speaking. Number two is death. Death is number two. Does that sound right? This means to the average person, if you go to a funeral, you're better off in the casket than doing the eulogy.

—Jerry Seinfeld

BY NINA LESOWITZ

Have you ever turned down a promotion because it involved public speaking? Do you live with regrets about keeping silent during a memorial for a loved one? Get sick to your stomach just thinking about standing up in front of a group of people?

I have experienced all of those feelings—plus panic, paralysis, and uncontrollable trembling. Although I read up on the latest studies associated with the fear of public speaking, and was aware of how common it is, I still felt alone and isolated. People always expressed disbelief when

I described how terrified I was to speak in front of a group. I often felt I was the only person I knew who had this problem. I was in awe of others' ability to seem relaxed, and even funny, when speaking in public. I thought it was a skill that I would never learn, that there was something intrinsically wrong with me.

Of course, I was not alone, although I spent a lot of time trying to figure out the source of this fear. Looking into it didn't make it better. It only grew worse over time.

I found comfort knowing that many, many studies have been conducted on this subject. In one study, 80 percent of respondents said they would rather face imminent death than speak in front of a large crowd of people. And another study showed that 40 percent of people were so afraid to speak in public that they could safely say they would never consider a position where it was necessary.

Fear of public speaking strikes some people harder, and differently, than others, according to a new study. The study shows that those who suffer most over speaking in public grow more anxious—not less anxious—as their presentation gets under way. And when it's over, instead of feeling relief, they feel even more anxious.

Although it has always been my goal to write books, I postponed my second book because I knew I would have to promote it. (I hid behind my co-author during our first book tour.) Many years ago, I chose public relations as a profession because I thought I was more comfortable being behind the scenes. I never gave myself a chance.

Whether organizing an event, a speaking engagement, or a media interview, I was always presenting someone else's point of view. In fact, I give clients tips for how to put their best foot forward on camera, but I sidestepped the spotlight whenever it came anywhere near me.

After co-authoring the book *Living Life as a Thank You* in 2009, I knew that I would have to give presentations at my scheduled book signings, and also do live interviews for TV and other media.

I finally had no choice but to tackle my fear head on. In October 2009, I joined Toastmasters, an international nonprofit organization that helps people become more competent and comfortable in front of an audience. I joined a group in downtown Oakland, California, that includes many accomplished people, including Michael Notaro, the second vice president for Toastmasters International. (He will likely be international president elect after August 2010.) Michael has been a member of Toastmasters since May 1985, when he was a student at the University of California, Berkeley, and wanted to prepare for a graduation speech.

"Presentation skills are crucial to success in the workplace," Michael says. "Many people pay high fees to coaches to gain the skill and confidence necessary to face an audience. Toastmasters provides an option that is less expensive and is proven effective." The organization has been around for more than 85 years and offers a proven—and enjoyable—way to practice and hone communication and leadership skills.

Michael gives so many stellar speeches, but I particularly remember one he gave when I first joined. It made me think about the benefits of Toastmasters beyond the ability to structure my speeches and watch out for "ahs" and "ums." He made me realize that once you go through this program, you can acquire a sense of confidence that will make you say, "Yes, I can" to much more than public speaking.

It's a huge leap for me, coming out from behind the scenes for my long-delayed time in the sun.

POWER PRACTICE

Many of us have beliefs that prevent us from fully living up to our potential. Those beliefs, which live in our subconscious, are generated by fear. We think, There is something wrong with me, and therefore I cannot speak in public, or introduce myself to strangers, or drive a car.

It takes courage to accept that avoiding these fears doesn't make them go away. By facing these fears, by joining an organization like Toastmasters, for example, we learn from them. Every time we face a fear honestly and ask for support from others, it gets better, a little bit at a time. This frees us from limitations, and allows us to be who we are truly meant to be.

RECOMMENDED INSPIRATIONAL READING

This is just a small sampling of books written by or about some very courageous people who have inspired us. They are listed in no particular order.

Long Walk to Freedom: The Autobiography of Nelson Mandela, by Nelson Mandela (Back Bay Books, 1995)

Gandhi, an Autobiography: The Story of My Experiments with Truth, by Mohandas Karamchand Gandhi (Beacon Press, 1993)

Harriet Tubman: The Road to Freedom, by Catherine Clinton (Back Bay Books, 2005)

Let's Roll! Ordinary People, Extraordinary Courage, by Lisa Beamer (Tyndale House Publishers, 2006)

A World Made New: Eleanor Roosevelt and the Universal Declaration of Human Rights, by Mary Ann Glendon (Random House, 2002)

In My Hands: Memories of a Holocaust Rescuer, by Irene Opdyke (Laurel Leaf, 2004)

Martin Luther King Jr.: A Life, by Marshall Frady (Penguin, 2005)

It's Not About the Bike: My Journey Back to Life, by Lance Armstrong and Sally Jenkins (Berkley Trade, 2001)

Cruelest Journey: Six Hundred Miles to Timbuktu, by Kira Salak (National Geographic, 2004)

Into Africa: The Epic Adventures of Stanley and Livingstone, by Martin Dugard (Broadway, 2004)

Rosa Parks: My Story, by Rosa Parks and Jim Haskins (Puffin, 1999)

Mother Teresa: Come Be My Light, by Mother Teresa and Brian Kolodiejchuk (Doubleday, 2007)

Night, by Elie Wiesel (Hill and Wang, revised edition, 2006)

Between a Rock and a Hard Place, by Aron Ralston (Atria, 2005)

Into Thin Air: A Personal Account of the Mt. Everest Disaster, by Jon Krakauer (Anchor, 2009)

Failure Is Impossible: Susan B. Anthony in Her Own Words, by Lynn Sherr (Times Books, 1996)

Endurance: Shackleton's Incredible Voyage, by Alfred Lansing (Carroll & Graf, 1999)

True North: Peary, Cook, and the Race to the Pole, by Bruce Henderson (W.W. Norton & Co., 2006)

Luckiest Man: The Life and Death of Lou Gehrig, by Jonathan Eig (Simon & Schuster, 2006)

Notorious Victoria: The Life of Victoria Woodhull, Uncensored, by Mary Gabriel (Algonquin Books, 1998)

Resilience: Reflections on the Burdens and Gifts of Facing Life's Adversities, by Elizabeth Edwards (Broadway, 2009)

Easy Company Soldier: The Legendary Battles of a Sergeant from World War II's "Band of Brothers," by Don Malarkey (St. Martin's Griffin, 2009)

Our War for the World: A Memoir of Life and Death on the Front Lines in WW II, by Brendon Phibbs (Lyons Press, 2002)

Breaking Trail: A Climbing Life, by Arlene Blum (Harvest Books, 2007)

Gorillas in the Mist: A Remarkable Story of Thirteen Years Spent Living with the Greatest of the Great Apes, by Dian Fossey (Phoenix, 2001)

ABOUT THE AUTHORS

Photo: Peter Diggs

NINA LESOWITZ is a public relations practitioner and author who has been featured on national, state, and local television and radio as well as in newspaper and magazine articles. She served as a resident expert on PBS.org in 2010. Born in Brooklyn, New York, Nina has traveled extensively throughout the world and witnessed many acts of courageousness firsthand. She is the co-author of two bestselling books: *The Party Girl Cookbook* and, with Mary Beth Sammons, *Living Life as a Thank You*. Nina lives in Piedmont, California, with her husband, Martin, and two daughters.

Photo: Suzanne Plunkett Photographs

MARY BETH SAMMONS is an award-winning journalist and author who writes about health, wellness, and reinventing your life in various print and online health and wellness sites such as AOL Health and the *Chicago Tribune*. She is a former bureau chief for *Crain's Chicago Business* and is the author of nine books, among them *Second Acts That*

Change Lives: Making a Difference in the World and *My Family: Collected Memories.* She has received several industry awards, including first place from United Press International for best spot news coverage, a PR Silver Anvil Award, and an undergraduate scholarship from the William Randolph Hearst Foundation. She lives in the Chicago area with her three children.

TO OUR READERS

Viva Editions publishes books that inform, enlighten, and entertain. We do our best to bring you, the reader, quality books that celebrate life, inspire the mind, revive the spirit, and enhance lives all around. Our authors are practical visionaries: people who offer deep wisdom in a hopeful and helpful manner. Viva was launched with an attitude of growth and we want to spread our joy and offer our support and advice where we can to help you live the Viva way: vivaciously!

We're grateful for all our readers and want to keep bringing you books for inspired living. We invite you to write to us with your comments and suggestions, and what you'd like to see more of. You can also sign up for our online newsletter to learn about new titles, author events, and special offers.

Viva Editions
2246 Sixth St.
Berkeley, CA 94710
www.vivaeditions.com
(800) 780-2279
Follow us on Twitter @vivaeditions
Friend/fan us on Facebook